Fit for Purpose

A Lenten Course in Spiritual Health

ED HONE

kevin mayhew

kevin
mayhew

First published in Great Britain in 2012 by Kevin Mayhew Ltd
Buxhall, Stowmarket, Suffolk IP14 3BW
Tel: +44 (0) 1449 737978 Fax: +44 (0) 1449 737834
E-mail: info@kevinmayhewltd.com

www.kevinmayhew.com

ISBN 978 1 84867 542 1
Catalogue No. 1501366

Cover design by Rob Mortonson
© Images used under licence from Shutterstock Inc.
Edited by Nicki Copeland
Typeset by Richard Weaver

Printed and bound in Great Britain

Contents

About the author

Ed Hone is a member of the Redemptorist missionary order. He specialises in mission development, preaching, and creative liturgy, working chiefly in Britain and Ireland. Ed is currently parish priest of the English-speaking Catholic parish in Luxembourg.

Introduction

Lent is a special, privileged time when we pause for thought and prayer, to reflect on our lives in the light of the gospel. The traditional 40 days are based on the time Jesus spent in the desert, being tempted and being prepared for his ministry and for his suffering and death. This year, we are looking at our spiritual fitness – not to see whether we are spiritual hares or tortoises, but to see how much in accord we are with the purposes of our loving God. This book is not an instruction manual, even less a book of rules that you must follow. It is rather a resource, something you and your house or church group can use to assist your reflection, discussion and prayer. You can adapt it to suit your needs, miss out what's not helpful, and add anything you think might be missing. Although written primarily for groups, it can easily be adapted for individual use.

Lent is a somewhat austere season, but it is always a privileged season. Even though our thoughts are more on the Lord's temptation, Passion and death, for us, all this is in the light of the resurrection. The Lamb, once slain, lives for ever! So let's apply ourselves to the task of reflecting, personally and with each other's help, asking for God's help and grace.

Each week follows the same pattern and comprises a number of elements. Two outlines are presented here: the first is for group use; the second for those who wish to follow the course by themselves.

How to use *Fit for Purpose* in a group

Notes for leaders

The elements below may be followed as presented, or adapted according to circumstances.

Catching up: It is important here to be sensitive to the nature of the group. A group of people who know each other well may possibly chat more freely and on a more personal level. Groups where people do not know each other well may partake in more general, less personal sharing until they feel comfortable with more. If there is potentially inappropriate disclosure (e.g. someone making themselves vulnerable, or simply gossiping) the leader is advised to steer the conversation in a different direction. The leader can also ensure that anyone who wishes to speak is given a chance to, and that anyone who is reluctant to share does not feel pressured into doing so. And, of course, the leader will remind the group that 'what is said in the group stays in the group'. Confidentiality is vital in order for trust to be maintained.

The matter in hand: This is best read individually by all members of the group *before* the meeting, to enable time for personal reflection. Five or ten minutes may be given during the meeting for a rereading (or a first-time reading for those who did not manage to prepare in advance).

Takeaway: A daily thought and prayer for each day of the coming week is given in the Appendix. These may be printed out on slips of paper and distributed to the group, or the group may simply be referred to the appropriate page of the Appendix.

Suggested format for the meeting

1. **Calming down:** An invitation to be still and become aware of the presence of the Lord (2-3 minutes). The invitation may be read out loud by the leader or another reader.
2. **Catching up:** The people are welcomed and invited by the leader to share what the past week has been like, what sorrows, joys and concerns they bring with them, and perhaps something they would like to ask of the Lord (5 minutes).
3. **Opening prayer:** To be read out loud by the leader or another reader.
4. **The matter in hand:** An introduction to the theme of the evening. Ideally, this reflection should be read by each group member in advance of the meeting. During the meeting, this time can be used by those present to reread it (individually) and refresh their memories (10 minutes).
5. **The word of the Lord:** the Scripture reading/s. Preferably, the reading will first be read out loud, and then a period of silence will be observed to enable those present to read it privately.
6. **Reflection:** A short reflection is read out and is followed by a time of silence (5 minutes).
7. **Talk-talk:** The leader invites group discussion on the theme. The questions provided may be used in whole or in part, or may be omitted if you prefer (15 minutes).

8. **Resolve:** Decide whether any practical action needs to be taken as a result of this reflection.
9. **Before the Lord:** A time of prayer, using the prayers and Scriptures supplied (to be read aloud), the suggested hymns and songs, and free prayer if desired (10 minutes).
10. **Takeaway:** Group members may be referred to the relevant Takeaway section of the Appendix, or a slip of paper may be given to each group member with the daily thoughts and short prayers for the week to come (see Appendix).
11. **Blessing:** A prayer is said together, asking God to bless the members of the group.

How to use *Fit for Purpose* by yourself

Using *Fit for Purpose* by yourself (i.e. not in a group) requires simple adaptation:

- Omit the group activities such as discussion.
- Change plurals such as *we* and *us* to *I* and *me.*
- In the prayers, simply ignore *Leader*, *All* and *Reader* and read the prayers and readings for yourself.
- Adjust the timings of each section as you feel appropriate.

1. **Calming down:** A time of stillness to become aware of the presence of the Lord.
2. **Catching up:** An opportunity to reflect on the past week and its events, sorrows and joys, and perhaps to call to mind any special prayer intentions.
3. **Opening prayer.**
4. **The matter in hand:** An introduction to the theme of the week; this can be read through slowly and reflectively.
5. **The word of the Lord:** The Scripture reading, which can be read through slowly and reflectively.
6. **Reflection:** A short reflection, ideally followed by a time of silence.
7. **Talk-talk:** The questions provided may be used to help in personal reflection, or they may be omitted.
8. **Resolve:** Decide whether any practical action needs to be taken as a result of this reflection.
9. **Before the Lord:** A time of prayer, using the prayers supplied.

10. **Takeaway:** The Appendix suggests a thought and a prayer for each day of the coming week.
11. **Blessing:** To be prayed silently.

Appendix

These additional resources at the back of the book offer helpful additions for the meetings and individuals during the week:

- **Takeaway:** A thought and a prayer for each day which may be printed out and distributed each week at the group meetings.
- **Spiritual diet sheet:** Questions to assist reflection on spiritual diet.
- **Praying the word of God:** Suggestions for praying the word at home.
- **Spiritual fitness quiz:** A light-hearted assessment of the state of our spiritual health.
- **Music for meditation:** A selection of instrumental music which might assist reflection.

Hymn/song numbers refer to *Anglican Hymns Old & New.*[1]

1. *Anglican Hymns Old & New*, Kevin Mayhew, 2008.

Week by week

The course runs from Ash Wednesday through to Easter Sunday, offering seven weekly sessions:

1. We are what we eat: a healthy spiritual diet
2. Exercising the heart: loving and living
3. Losing the baggage: letting go of what's weighing us down
4. Onwards and upwards: living prayerfully
5. Giving and not counting the cost: the grateful life
6. A helping hand: encouraging each other
7. Fit for a king: being a people of praise

The course may be commenced any time during the week of Ash Wednesday. The daily thoughts and prayers provided in the Appendix, whilst related to the theme of each week, are not necessarily day specific.

Week one

We are what we eat: a healthy spiritual diet

1. Calming down *(pause after each sentence)*

Leader: Let our minds and our bodies be still now. We are with each other, and the Lord is in our midst. God is the unseen guest whose presence brings peace, whose word nourishes our souls and holds out to us the promise of eternal life. God is within each of us the 'still small voice of calm'.

2. Catching up

Leader: Let us think for a few moments of all that has happened in our lives over the last week: the things we've done, the people we've met, the places we've visited. And we think of what's been on our minds: the worries and cares, the things that have made us smile, the news we want to pass on. We have a chance over the next few minutes to share that with each other – this is the 'me' I have brought here this evening, the 'me' I bring before the Lord.

3. Opening prayer

All: Your Spirit has gathered us in this place, Lord Jesus.
We welcome you into our midst, our honoured guest.
Take from us, we pray, all our care and woe,
and grant us peace.

May our ears be open to hear your word,
may our minds be helped to understand your teaching,
may our hearts be willing to embrace your truth,
may our spirits always sing your praise.
Amen.

4. The matter in hand – a healthy spiritual diet

In 1740, Vice Admiral Edward Vernon ordered that lime juice be added to the traditional navy tipple of rum and water in all the ships under his command. Although the juice was added to sweeten the often foul-tasting water on board, it was soon observed that sailors under Vernon's command were markedly healthier than sailors under other commanders. Seven years later, in one of the first ever clinical trials, Scottish physician James Lind proved that citrus juices (including lime) prevent scurvy – a common disease amongst sailors at sea.

Now we take for granted the need for a balanced diet, the need to take all the vitamins, minerals, proteins, fats, carbohydrates, sugars and water in their proper proportions, and we are much more aware of the effects of our diet on our health. We look also to balance other aspects of life too: work, rest, recreation, ongoing education and relationships. Less obvious, perhaps, is the balance of the spiritual aspects of our lives: our values, our aspirations, the beliefs that help us interpret the world and understand our place in it – and our relationship with God. Our spiritual diet is important.

What would an unbalanced diet look like? Well, we might be too busy rushing around helping people and neglect to pray for them as well. We might pray for this and for that and forget to do anything to try and help make things better. We might spend so much time at church services and meetings that we don't pay enough attention to our family. We might read lots of spiritual books but hardly ever read the Bible. There are so many ways we could get it wrong when, with a little attention, we could actually get it about right. What should we Christians 'eat', then, to nourish our spirits? And how do we find balance?

Of course, the Bible is central. In the Scriptures we have poetry, history, wisdom, teaching, law, instruction, visions, prophecy and biography. The whole rich story of God's engagement with humanity is to be found here. We learn about God, about the world, about our place in creation, about the promise held out to us of salvation in Jesus Christ. We can read the word of God alone, reflect on it with others, reflect on it prayerfully, study it, pray prayers woven from it, listen to sermons based on it – what is important is that we encounter the Lord in the word of God. There is a wealth of books on every aspect of the Christian life – books that can be useful to inspire, educate and guide us. We can share with our friends what has helped us, and listen to their recommendations too.

Our balanced diet includes personal prayer, through which we maintain our own relationship with God and through which we remain in touch with the One who is the source of our being, our Creator, our Saviour and the One who makes us holy.

Worshipping together has a vital place, too: it is when we truly are the people we are created to be, giving thanks and praise to God. Here we sing psalms, hymns and songs and hear God's word as a community, and in our Eucharist we follow the command of Jesus to 'Do this in memory of me'.

We can learn so much by studying and imitating the lives of holy men and women who have gone before us, and those who live in our midst; we can be inspired, encouraged, uplifted, strengthened and assisted by realising we are not alone, or even just part of a group: we are a people, chosen, royal, made holy by God's grace.

It would be a strange spiritual diet where there was no place for beauty: for poetry, literature, theatre, art, music and the natural world – anything that speaks to us of the restless creativity of God, that gives us a glimpse of heaven, that lifts us out of our everyday lives for even a moment. If we imagine that God is hidden and is trying to burst through to communicate with us and that all we have to do is to be attentive, alert, sensitive and attuned, we will find God in many unexpected places.

Many of our churches celebrate the seasons of Lent and Advent, and feast-days, all of which keep before us the mysteries of our salvation and hallow the months and the years. This diet, when balanced, enriches us spiritually, helps us grow in the Lord and fits us for heaven.

How do we score?

One thing to remember here is that the spiritual life is not a competition, a beauty pageant or a pass-or-fail exam. However, there are ways in which we can look at ourselves and see whether or not we are attending sufficiently to our spiritual health. One traditional way of doing this, which is especially suitable during our Lenten preparation for Easter, is the examination of conscience: a prayerful look at our life in the light of a Scripture passage or the gospel as a whole. Where we have fallen short of what God wants of us, we can ask forgiveness of God and of each other.

Another traditional method of auditing ourselves spiritually is to have an occasional review of life (often referred to as *revisio vitae*) where, either on our own or with the guidance of someone else, we look at the whole direction of our life and our faithfulness to God's call. Having a conversation with a trusted, wise church leader or member (*spiritual direction*) can help us look at ourselves and see where we need to grow. The Appendix includes a Spiritual diet sheet questionnaire to help you look at the balance of your spiritual diet, either alone or as a group.

Forbidden fruit – what's *not* good for us

Unfortunately, ensuring a balanced diet isn't just about consuming what's good for us, but it's also about forgoing what's not good – especially that which is positively harmful. Unfortunately, we are often attracted to and enjoy what's not good for us, even when we know it's doing us harm. In spiritual terms, it is best that we avoid the following (you can add to the list, of course):

- Sin, in all its manifestations (needless to say!)
- Sanctimoniousness, where we see ourselves as spiritually elite in some way
- Excessive legalism, where we live under law rather than grace
- Superstition, which is at best a distraction in our faith
- 'Unhelpful' media (books, films, etc.) that bring out the worst in us or reduce us in some way.

No one said the spiritual diet was easy!

5. The word of the Lord

Leader or another reader: The apostles gathered around Jesus, and told him all that they had done and taught. He said to them, 'Come away to a deserted place all by yourselves and rest a while.' For many were coming and going, and they had no leisure even to eat. And they went away in the boat to a deserted place by themselves. Now many saw them going and recognised them, and they hurried there on foot from all the towns and arrived ahead of them. As he went ashore, he

saw a great crowd; and he had compassion for them, because they were like sheep without a shepherd; and he began to teach them many things. When it grew late, his disciples came to him and said, 'This is a deserted place, and the hour is now very late; send them away so that they may go into the surrounding country and villages and buy something for themselves to eat.' But he answered them, 'You give them something to eat.' They said to him, 'Are we to go and buy two hundred denarii worth of bread, and give it to them to eat?' And he said to them, 'How many loaves have you? Go and see.' When they had found out, they said, 'Five, and two fish.' Then he ordered them to get all the people to sit down in groups on the green grass. So they sat down in groups of hundreds and of fifties. Taking the five loaves and the two fish, he looked up to heaven, and blessed and broke the loaves, and gave them to his disciples to set before the people; and he divided the two fish among them all. And all ate and were filled; and they took up twelve baskets full of broken pieces and of the fish. Those who had eaten the loaves numbered five thousand men.
Mark 6:30-44

6. Reflection

Leader: The ministry of Jesus was extraordinarily rich and varied: he taught, he healed, he forgave sin, he befriended, he preached, he reproached, he blessed – and he fed! There was no one-size-fits-all salvation; rather, Jesus responded to each person according to their need; in the presence of Jesus, there was, and is, something for everyone. In this time of quiet, let us reflect on what it is that we need from the Lord. We approach him in prayer, and we ask, simply and directly. And then we give thanks.

The time of reflection is brought to an end by the leader simply saying, 'Amen'.

7. Talk-talk

- What are the most important ingredients in a spiritual diet? Are these the same for everybody?
- Should our spiritual diet change over time, or depending on circumstances?
- Can we add any ingredients that have not been mentioned so far?
- What is our local church good at providing? What is missing?
- How do we supplement our spiritual diet?
- What kinds of 'symptoms' might be apparent if our spiritual life is not balanced?

8. Resolve

Decide whether any practical action needs to be taken as a result of this reflection.

9. Before the Lord

Suggested hymns and songs, if desired:
5000 + hungry folk (188)
Gather around, for the table is spread (213)
Christ is the heavenly food (98)

Leader: He said to them, 'Come away to a deserted place all by yourselves and rest a while' (Mark 6:31).

Leader: Let us still ourselves once again, as we pray.

All: Let us listen to the Lord's voice in our hearts.

Pause

Psalm 1

All: Happy are those
who do not follow the advice of the wicked,
or take the path that sinners tread,
or sit in the seat of scoffers;
but their delight is in the law of the Lord,
and on his law they meditate day and night.
They are like trees
planted by streams of water,
which yield their fruit in its season,
and their leaves do not wither.
In all that they do, they prosper.

The wicked are not so,
but are like chaff that the wind drives away.
Therefore the wicked will not stand in the judgement,
nor sinners in the congregation of the righteous;
for the Lord watches over the way of the righteous,
but the way of the wicked will perish.

Scripture verse

(to be read out loud again, with pause for reflection)

He said to them, 'Come away to a deserted place all by yourselves and rest a while' (Mark 6:31).

Pause

Petitions

(to be read aloud by the leader or another reader; pause after each)

Let us ask the Lord for a spirit of prayer.
Let us ask the Lord for peace in our hearts and in our world.
Let us ask the Lord for healing and wholeness.

We pray that we might always be open to God's word.
We pray that we might be generous to those in need.
We pray that we might comfort those who are sad.

Let us ask the Lord that we might grow in faith.
Let us ask the Lord that we might truly live the gospel.
Let us ask the Lord to bless our churches.

Other petitions may be added.

Leader: Lord, teach us your way.
All: Teach us how we should love.

Leader: Lord, help us to grow.
All: Help us to be more like you.

Leader: Lord, lead us on the path of true life.
All: Lead us to eternal life.

Leader: Be near us this day and every day.
All: Be near us to give us strength, courage and peace.

Our Father . . .

10. Takeaway

A thought and a prayer for each day, which you might find of help, until we meet again *(see Appendix).*

11. Blessing

All: You have blessed us all, Lord, in each other.
You have blessed us with your presence.
You have blessed us with your word.
Bless us all once again, we ask you,
and bless those whom we love, this night and always.
Amen.

Week two

Exercising the heart: loving and living

1. Calming down *(pause after each sentence)*

Leader: We think of our homes, our families, the people who make up our lives. Then we gradually narrow our focus to this place, to the people we are with here. There is one guest we cannot see, but who assures us of his presence whenever two or three of us gather in his name: Jesus Christ. For a few moments, let us ponder his presence in our midst.

2. Catching up

Leader: Let us think for a few moments of all that has happened in our lives over the last week: the things we've done, the people we've met, the places we've visited. And we think of what's been on our minds: the worries and cares, the things that have made us smile, the news we want to pass on. We have a chance over the next few minutes to share that with each other – this is the 'me' I have brought here this evening, the 'me' I bring before the Lord.

3. Opening prayer

All: Lord, we have come together
to discuss, to reflect and to pray,
to be guided by your Holy Spirit.
We ask that we may listen attentively to your voice
in our hearts and through each other
so that we might hear
what you wish to teach us.

You have given us a life-giving word,
and for this we give you thanks and praise.
Amen.

4. The matter in hand – loving and living

We're well aware of the seven colours of the rainbow, even though it's not always possible to distinguish them all when we see a rainbow in the sky. Light, however, is much more complex than the light-splitting qualities of a prism might lead us to believe. At one end of the spectrum, invisible to the human eye, is infrared. It is used in TV remote controls and night-vision cameras, amongst other everyday items. At the other end is ultraviolet, the element in sunlight that can be so damaging to our skin but which stimulates plants to grow.

We face a similar, if more profound, complexity when we try to define love. We can say what its opposite is, and we can make a good guess as to what love is *not*. But trying to say what love actually *is* presents us with a challenge. If love is important in life and in faith, though, we have to make an attempt – and love is indeed important. We are told in the Bible that God is love.[2] We believe that Jesus was sent because 'God so loved the world'.[3] We are told that Jesus was loved by his heavenly Father[4] and gave his life on the cross out of love for humanity. And we have his command to 'love one another. Just as I have loved you . . .'[5]

There's no shirking – we need to get to grips with this love thing, and there's no better place for us to start than with Jesus himself.

---

2. 1 John 4:8.
3. John 3:16.
4. John 3:35.
5. John 13:34.

The love of Jesus

What was the love of Jesus like? How did he show it? It's here that we begin to see the complexity of love: it manifests in so many ways. Jesus always desired the well-being of others, and was 'moved with compassion' by their suffering.[6] He was patient with those who made demands on him, exhausting himself as he taught the crowds; he spoke the truth even when it was difficult for his hearers to receive; he showed no prejudice, even defying social and religious convention to respect the dignity of others, whether lepers, adulterers or cheats. Perhaps the supreme aspect of his love, and the most obviously recognisable to us, is his gift of himself for the life of the world.

Jesus spoke of love, desired his disciples to live in love, and in his life and death demonstrated love. For Jesus, love was not simply a virtue to be practised or a way of being holy and pleasing to God; it was, and is, the key to living a full life. John in his letters reflects on this at length: living in love is living in God, and God lives in the person who lives in love. That is an amazing truth, a wonderful gift, and an awesome responsibility. How do we live in love? One clue is in living in conscious awareness of the love God has shown us, and still shows. We'll be looking at this more closely in week 5.

The key here is not the obvious one of 'What would Jesus do?' which is, of course, worthy, but it doesn't go far enough; it isn't sufficient – and it can be a distraction. Our real focus is to live 'in Christ'.

Life 'in Christ'

Paul has a remarkable notion of what it means to be a Christian: it is to be 'in Christ'. He refers to two fellow

6. Matthew 20:34.

apostles who were 'in Christ before I was'[7] and says that, 'as all die in Adam, so all will be made alive in Christ'.[8] Paul writes to the church in Corinth 'to those who are sanctified in Christ Jesus, called to be saints . . .'[9] His use of language is quite distinctive. He does not speak of being 'in the church', nor even of being 'in the church of Christ', but of being 'in Christ'. All will be made alive not 'by Christ' but 'in Christ'. We are made holy not 'by Christ' but 'in Christ'. So when we are fully 'in Christ', we see with the eyes of Christ, think with the mind of Christ, love with the heart of Christ, serve with the humility of Christ. This is so much more than trying to imagine what he would do and then seeking to do likewise.

How can we be 'in Christ'? Is it a technique, or something that happens automatically – say, with baptism? The answer is that when we live in the Spirit of Christ, we have, as Paul says, 'the mind of Christ'.[10] We are in Christ as individuals and as community. And if we have the mind of Christ, we can love with the love of Christ and act in the name of Christ. This way, what we do, say and think is coming from the risen Lord himself, though inevitably filtered through our sinful nature. Being in Christ draws us further and further into him; then as we exercise our heart, loving and truly living, we reinforce our closeness to him. We are attending to our spiritual health, and becoming the people God always intended us to be.

Here are some practical suggestions to help us live 'in Christ'. Firstly, we pray for the help of the Holy Spirit, without whom we can do nothing. Secondly, we immerse ourselves in Christ when we pray – with Jesus, to the Father,

---

7. Romans 16:7.
8. 1 Corinthians 15:22.
9. 1 Corinthians 1:2.
10. 1 Corinthians 2:16.

in the Spirit. It therefore follows that the more attentive we are to prayer, the more we will be drawn into Christ (bearing in mind the need for a balanced spiritual diet that we considered last week). Thirdly, we immerse ourselves in the word of God in the Scriptures. When we do this, again with the Spirit's help, we enter into the good news of the risen Christ. Through our immersion in Scripture, especially in the Gospels, we come to know not just what Jesus said and did but we also begin to understand more fully *how* and *why*. We begin to understand from the inside, and his way becomes, over time and with the help of grace, our way. If we become discouraged at our lack of conformity to the way of Jesus, or if we doubt in some way that we are 'in Christ', we mustn't give up. This is where we can help, encourage, challenge, affirm and learn from each other.

5. The word of the Lord

Leader or another reader: Philip said to him, 'Lord, show us the Father, and we will be satisfied.' Jesus said to him, 'Have I been with you all this time, Philip, and you still do not know me? Whoever has seen me has seen the Father. How can you say, "Show us the Father"? Do you not believe that I am in the Father and the Father is in me? The words that I say to you I do not speak on my own; but the Father who dwells in me does his works. Believe me that I am in the Father and the Father is in me; but if you do not, then believe me because of the works themselves. Very truly, I tell you, the one who believes in me will also do the works that I do and, in fact, will do greater works than these, because I am going to the Father. I will do whatever you ask in my name, so that the Father may be glorified in the Son. If in my name you ask me for anything, I will do it.

'If you love me, you will keep my commandments. And I will ask the Father, and he will give you another Advocate, to be with you for ever. This is the Spirit of truth, whom the world cannot receive, because it neither sees him nor knows him. You know him, because he abides with you, and he will be in you. I will not leave you orphaned; I am coming to you. In a little while the world will no longer see me, but you will see me; because I live, you also will live. On that day you will know that I am in my Father, and you in me, and I in you.'
John 14:8-20

6. Reflection

Leader: The challenge for us as disciples is to live in Christ, to live in the love of Christ, and so to show Christ to the world. This is how we witness, individually and together, to the gospel. Our witness isn't necessarily talking about Jesus or God or church all the time; it's firstly living and loving in a gospel way. In our reflection now we acknowledge once again the presence of Christ in our midst. We think prayerfully about our life 'in Christ', and about how we can encourage each other in faith. If you think it would be helpful, you could repeat over and again silently, 'Thank you, Lord, for calling me to live in your love,' or, 'Help me, Lord, to live in your love.'

The time of reflection is brought to an end by the leader simply saying, 'Amen'.

7. Talk-talk

- What is my chief witness to Christ in my life?
- What are the challenges in loving as Christ loves?

- Do we prefer the idea of 'What would Jesus do?' to the idea of being 'in Christ'? Why/why not?
- Is there anything that strikes you from the passage from John 14? Is there anything you haven't noticed before, or have heard in a new way?
- What does the passage mean to you? Can you relate to it?
- Would you like to attempt to make a definition of love?

8. Resolve

Decide whether any practical action needs to be taken as a result of this reflection.

9. Before the Lord

Suggested hymns and songs, if desired:
Come, gracious Spirit, heavenly Dove (122)
Such love (681)
A new commandment (4)

Leader: 'And remember, I am with you always, to the end of the age' (Matthew 28:20).

Leader: When we had lost our way and could not obey
All: Christ came to show us the way to love.

Leader: When we were deaf to the voice of the prophets
All: Christ came to show us the way to the Father.

Leader: When we could not live the law of the Lord
All: Christ came to teach us the heart of the law.

Leader: When we were enemies with God and with each other
All: Christ came to bring us peace.

Leader: When we felt sullied with sin
All: Christ came to bring us forgiveness.

Leader: When we imagined God to be distant and aloof
All: Christ came to bring God close.

Leader: When we were afraid of being left alone
All: Christ came, to remain with us to the end of the age.

All: We give thanks to you, O Christ, Holy One of God, for all the good things you have given us, even the gift of your own self.
Help us to live in your love and to share the good news of your reign. You who live and reign with the Father and the Holy Spirit.
Amen.

Psalm 29

Leader 2: A Psalm of David.
Ascribe to the Lord, O heavenly beings,
ascribe to the Lord glory and strength.
Ascribe to the Lord the glory of his name;
worship the Lord in holy splendour.

All: The voice of the Lord is over the waters;
the God of glory thunders,
the Lord, over mighty waters.
The voice of the Lord is powerful;
the voice of the Lord is full of majesty.

Leader 2: The voice of the Lord breaks the cedars;
the Lord breaks the cedars of Lebanon.
He makes Lebanon skip like a calf,
and Sirion like a young wild ox.

All: The voice of the Lord flashes forth flames of fire.
The voice of the Lord shakes the wilderness;
the Lord shakes the wilderness of Kadesh.

Leader 2: The voice of the Lord causes the oaks to whirl,
and strips the forest bare;
and in his temple all say, 'Glory!'

All: The Lord sits enthroned over the flood;
the Lord sits enthroned as king for ever.
May the Lord give strength to his people!
May the Lord bless his people with peace!

Scripture verse

(to be read out loud again, with pause for reflection)

'And remember, I am with you always, to the end of the age' (Matthew 28:20).

Petitions

(pause after each)

For the courage we need to share our faith with others,
for faith deeply rooted in Christ,
for the gift to see as Christ sees.

That we might support those who doubt,
that we might live in Christ's love,
that we might forgive as Christ forgives.

For this group present here, and those we love,
for all Christians, and all God's people,
for those we know who are suffering.

Other petitions may be added.

Leader: Let us live in love,
All: for when we live in love we live in God.

Leader: Let us serve one another,
All: imitating the Lord who came to serve.

Leader: Let us remain in peace
All: by the grace of the One who is our peace.

Our Father . . .

10. Takeaway

A thought and a prayer for each day, which you might find of help, until we meet again *(see Appendix)*.

11. Blessing

Leader 2: Blessed be God,
All: and blessed be God's kingdom of peace.

Leader 2: Blessed be God's creation,
All: and blessed be God's holy people.

Leader 2: Blessed be God, Father, Son and Spirit,
All: and may we be blessed by God. Amen.

Week three

Losing the baggage: letting go of what's weighing us down

1. Calming down *(pause after each sentence)*

Leader: In this time, we leave behind the cares of this day and rest in the presence of the Lord. The Lord, true to his promise, is in our midst – an accepting, forgiving and loving presence. For a few moments, in stillness, we open our hearts and minds to him.

2. Catching up

Leader: Let us think for a few moments of all that has happened in our lives over the last week: the things we've done, the people we've met, the places we've visited. And we think of what's been on our minds: the worries and cares, the things that have made us smile, the news we want to pass on. We have a chance over the next few minutes to share that with each other – this is the 'me' I have brought here this evening, the 'me' I bring before the Lord.

3. Opening prayer

All: Heavenly Father,
nothing is hidden
from your loving, merciful gaze,
and you know us just as we are.
You know our truth and untruth,
our strengths and our weaknesses,
our dreams and our fears,
our love and our lack of love.

Help us to grow in spirit,
that we might become
more like your Son Jesus,
our Saviour and our friend.
We ask this through the same Christ our Lord.
Amen.

4. The matter in hand – letting go of what's weighing us down

The arrival of cheap air travel in recent years has meant that millions of people are able to make journeys they would hardly have dreamed of making before. 'No-frills' airlines are just that: they provide the basics and charge extra for everything else. Carry-on baggage is restricted in size and weight, and hold luggage must be paid for by the bag or case. This means that most people travel more lightly than they might otherwise have done. Often it's not easy deciding what to pack and what to leave behind. And what's true of luggage is also true of our 'personal baggage' – the emotional, spiritual and psychological issues that are part of our make-up. This baggage can weigh us down and make us feel burdened, unfree, resentful, guilty, despondent or ashamed. This isn't good for our spiritual health, and it's not how things are meant to be. The Lord who came to bring us fullness of life[11] doesn't wish for us to be impeded in this way.

It would be useful for us to reflect on where this baggage comes from. Is it inherited, part of our genetic coding, an inevitable part of life? Is it something that other people, deliberately or unwittingly, foist upon us? Are we stuck with it, or is there something we can do about it?

11. See John 10:10.

The answer to the question, 'Where do our issues come from?' is straightforward, if not particularly helpful: all over the place! There are psychological conditions and predispositions that we are born with that may, for example, mean we are likely to be anxious. Sometimes these are curable or treatable, sometimes not. Much of who and how we are is a result of 'nurture' rather than 'nature', a result of our upbringing, our experience of life and the choices we have made. And some of who and how we are is mysterious – we have no idea where it comes from.

As we're dealing here with *spiritual* health, we'll consider mostly our spiritual baggage and what can be done about it.

Firstly, we'll think about the original issue, the big one, the one that had us expelled by God from Paradise: sin, with its effects, the burdens it places upon us and the sure remedy that is available to us. According to Augustine, we are all tainted with the sin of Adam and Eve. Even if we didn't believe this, we would have to acknowledge that there seems to be no way of escaping human sinfulness. We've yet to meet a truly sinless person. There is a fault line running through our nature that makes us behave as we shouldn't and prevents us from doing what we should, as Paul acknowledged.[12] We can't just sigh, though, and accept it as inevitable. We can face our sinfulness and struggle to live the life of grace, training our will to do what is good and to avoid what is not. The sure remedy for sin is forgiveness, where we call on the unfailing mercy of God. There is no sin that is unforgivable,[13] and it was precisely for sinners that Jesus came among us, and with sinners that he spent so much of his time.

12. See Romans 7:19.

13. Apart from the sin 'against the Holy Spirit' (Matthew 12:32) and as we can't be certain what that is, we can only watch out for what we think it might be, and move on.

How do we ask for God's forgiveness? Firstly, we examine our actions in the light of the gospel and acknowledge to ourselves where we have departed from God's way. We might reflect on *why* we did what we did and how we might avoid it next time. We might find it helpful to do something to show that we are genuinely sorry – even something that tries to put right the wrong we have done. Then in faith we ask God for forgiveness and peace; we can do this praying alone or with another person, perhaps a minister. And then, in the sure knowledge that our genuine request for forgiveness will be granted by God, we pray in thanksgiving. Doing this regularly can be helpful in honing our conscience and strengthening our will – but of course it shouldn't be obsessive or cause us anxiety.

Related to shedding the baggage of sin is, as we have just mentioned, dealing with the effects of sin. Where our anger has hurt someone, for example, we should try wherever possible to make amends; where we've taken something that's not ours, we should try to return it; where we haven't told the truth, we should seek to live in the truth. In this way, we shed the baggage of the after-effects of sin. And where we need help, there is no shame in speaking to someone we can trust about it: they can hardly judge, as they are a sinner too!

Whilst the next piece of baggage might be defined as sin, it's worth considering separately as sometimes it's unconscious and unintentional – but it's always potentially damaging: prejudice. This is where we take a mindset for or against something or someone, against reason and without proper knowledge, and close our minds. There's probably some kind of prejudice in us all, if we're honest. As baggage, it's not good for us to carry around and not good for those who bump into it. This is where we need to rewind to last week, to remember that we are 'in Christ', and to think with the mind of Christ. The more successfully we do this, the more we leave prejudice behind. And good riddance! Similarly resentment, envy, jealousy and the rest. Sometimes they're sin, sometimes they're like states of mind that we can't shake off and which hold us back. And again, the remedy is prayer, getting into good habits of mind, and evasive action; and, when all else fails, asking for forgiveness.

A powerful piece of baggage that can prove very difficult to let go of is regret: to wish that the past, and our actions in the past, had been different. Like all our other baggage, regret is a dead end: it goes nowhere and it can't change anything. But we can address it, and we should, if we are to be inwardly free. We must think of whatever it is that we regret and use it as our starting point for moving on, rather than it being the place where we end up. We give thanks for lessons we may have learned from the past and resolve not to forget them. And finally, we sing boldly, along with Edith Piaf, 'Je ne regrette rien' – I regret nothing. There's no point!

There's one more thing we're going to consider here: how we deal with other people's baggage; and the important thing is that we don't make it our own. It's all too easy for someone else's attitude or behaviour to have a negative effect on our own, where we react rather than respond. Again, we think with the mind of Christ. But in addition, we ask ourselves, 'Is there any way in which I can help make this person's burden lighter?' And is there any way in which I am responsible for how this person is? And finally, how best can I live gracefully with this person and their issues? As always, reflection on God's word is vital.

5. The word of the Lord

Leader or another reader: At that time Jesus said, 'I thank you, Father, Lord of heaven and earth, because you have hidden these things from the wise and the intelligent and have revealed them to infants; yes, Father, for such was your gracious will. All things have been handed over to me by my Father; and no one knows the Son except the Father, and no one knows the Father except the Son and anyone to whom the Son chooses to reveal him.

'Come to me, all you that are weary and are carrying heavy burdens, and I will give you rest. Take my yoke upon you, and learn from me; for I am gentle and humble in heart, and you will find rest for your souls. For my yoke is easy, and my burden is light.'
Matthew 11:25-30

As he was setting out on a journey, a man ran up and knelt before him, and asked him, 'Good Teacher, what must I do to inherit eternal life?' Jesus said to him, 'Why do you call me good? No one is good but God alone. You know the commandments: "You shall not murder; You shall not commit adultery; You shall not steal; You shall not bear false witness; You shall not defraud; Honour your father and mother."' He said to him, 'Teacher, I have kept all these since my youth.' Jesus, looking at him, loved him and said, 'You lack one thing; go, sell what you own, and give the money to the poor, and you will have treasure in heaven; then come, follow me.' When he heard this, he was shocked and went away grieving, for he had many possessions.
Mark 10:17-22

6. Reflection

Leader: The words from Matthew's Gospel speak of simplicity, consolation, encouragement and tender care. When life seems to get too complicated, we remember them. When we feel that the demands being made on us are too great, we keep them in mind. When we are lonely or afraid, we pray them. When we meet others who are in need, we share them.

The incident reported in Mark's Gospel equally emphasises simplicity of life, but in a different way. Jesus identifies the one thing that is missing from the rich man's life: simplicity. Clearly, the man's possessions were weighing him down and causing him spiritual unease – hence his question to the Lord. In the event, he was too attached to what he owned to embrace the radical command of Jesus. Jesus looked at the man and 'loved him'. This is the context for all that the Lord asks of us, and even when we feel we cannot live up to his commands, that love does not falter or diminish.

Here we might reflect upon what baggage we carry: what is weighing us down spiritually and preventing us from being truly free. We can imagine ourselves before the Lord and hearing his words, either from Matthew's Gospel or from Mark's.

The time of reflection is brought to an end by the leader simply saying, 'Amen'.

7. Talk-talk

- Can we identify what 'baggage' we carry?
- In what ways can we help each other with what holds us back spiritually?
- Religious belief can sometimes give us hang-ups (e.g. excessive guilt). How can we deal with this?

- Have we ever been helped or encouraged by the words of Jesus in Matthew 11 (above)?
- How might we respond to Jesus if he asked us to give up all our possessions and follow him? Why?
- Are there ways in which our faith helps us to deal with life? If so, what ways?
- What are regarded as the biggest sins today? Have these changed over the years?

8. Resolve

Decide whether any practical action needs to be taken as a result of this reflection.

9. Before the Lord

Suggested hymns and songs, if desired:
Come and celebrate (116)
All you who seek a comfort sure (28)
God forgave my sin (237)

Leader: 'For the law of the Spirit of life in Christ Jesus has set you free from the law of sin and of death' (Romans 8:2).

Psalm 131

All: O Lord, my heart is not lifted up,
my eyes are not raised too high;
I do not occupy myself with things
too great and too marvellous for me.
But I have calmed and quieted my soul,
like a weaned child with its mother;
my soul is like the weaned child that is with me.

O Israel, hope in the Lord
from this time on and for evermore.

Scripture verse

(to be read out loud again, with pause for reflection)

'For the law of the Spirit of life in Christ Jesus has set you free from the law of sin and of death' (Romans 8:2).

Leader: Let us ponder the ways in which Christ sets us free, and how we can do the same for others.

Petitions

Leader: When we know we have sinned,
when we have fallen short of the gospel of love,
when we are out of sorts with each other and the Lord,

All: Lord, we ask you to give us peace.
Lord, we ask for your forgiveness.
Lord, we ask you to make us whole.

Leader: When we are burdened with life's cares,
when we are weighed down with sadness,
when we are lost and confused,

All: We turn to you, Lord, because you are gentle and humble in heart.
We look to you, Lord, for your presence is our consolation.
We seek the guidance of your Holy Spirit.

Other petitions may be added.

Thanksgivings

Leader: When we know God's saving help,
when we are aware of the Lord's presence,
when the gospel gives us hope,

All: we give thanks and praise to you, Lord.
We offer you the worship of our hearts.
We acknowledge you to be our God.

Leader: When we experience the generosity of others,
when we hear a kindly word,
when those around us encourage us,

All: Lord, we praise your mercy.
Lord, we thank you for your goodness.
Lord, we glorify you. Amen.

Other thanksgivings may be added.

Our Father . . .

10. Takeaway

A thought and a prayer for each day, which you might find of help, until we meet again *(see Appendix)*.

11. Blessing

All: May the Lord who accompanies us on our journey guide us.
May the Lord who listens to us and teaches us, grant us wisdom.
May the Lord who guards us, bless us and those whom we love. Amen.

Week four

Onwards and upwards: living prayerfully

1. Calming down *(pause after each sentence)*

Leader: The Lord is with us, in our midst. In this time of quiet, we come before him and hand over to him all our cares and concerns, asking for his gift of peace. We are confident of his gentleness and his mercy.

2. Catching up

Leader: Let us think for a few moments of all that has happened in our lives over the last week: the things we've done, the people we've met, the places we've visited. And we think of what's been on our minds: the worries and cares, the things that have made us smile, the news we want to pass on. We have a chance over the next few minutes to share that with each other – this is the 'me' I have brought here this evening, the 'me' I bring before the Lord.

3. Opening prayer

All: Holy Spirit of God,
you live in us and you move freely and unseen
over the face of the earth.
You pray in us,
enabling us to address God as Father.
You inspire us and take away our fear,
helping us to proclaim
the good news of Jesus Christ.
Deepen in us the desire to pray,
our attentiveness to the word of God,
and a spirit of unity and peace.

We ask this of you,
who live and reign with the Father and the Son,
One God for ever and ever.
Amen.

4. The matter in hand – living prayerfully

At 02.36 on 21 July 1969[14] something momentous happened a long way away: a man stepped onto the moon. The words of that astronaut, Neil Armstrong, were heard all over the world: 'One small step for man, one giant leap for mankind.' Something which had belonged in the realm of science fiction a generation previously had now come to pass.

The moon landing was indeed a remarkable feat of science – and so was the technology that enabled words and images to be transmitted all the way back to earth. Less than 70 years earlier, Marconi was pioneering the sending of radio signals from one country to another, and then across the Atlantic from Europe to America. The rapid pace of scientific development that enabled the jump from international to interplanetary communication is amazing. Yet Christians are sharers in something even more incredible, something miraculous: prayer. In prayer, we communicate with a God who is not simply (in some senses) in a different place, but who is entirely *other*, different from us, even indescribable. Prayer is not a miracle of science but rather of grace: it is God's gift to us that we can communicate with, and even participate in, the very life of God.

Prayer and spiritual health

If we say that prayer is the means by which we live in God and God lives in us, we are some way towards understanding

14. Coordinated Universal Time (UTC).

how important it is. Without prayer at some level, we cannot flourish spiritually; indeed, we will waste away because we will be cut off from the source of our spiritual life. We'll look later on at how we pray. When prayer is a part of our spiritual diet – and we recognised the need for it to be in week 1 – then we are open to grow in faith, in wisdom and in hope, and to become more like the Lord who loves, gives and forgives. We don't pray, however, just because we need to, or because we should; we pray because it is part of who we are, who we were created to be: people in a relationship of love and thanksgiving with the God who made us. Prayer is in our nature, and when we don't pray we are going against part of our nature – and that can't be good!

What's going on when we pray?

A traditional definition of prayer is the 'raising of the heart and mind to God'. This isn't a bad definition, but it leaves a few gaps. The God to whom we pray is indeed 'up there' in heaven, but our prayer also needs to take into account the God who is present on earth, all around us and in our midst, deeply engaged with humanity. And as well as God being all around us, Paul tells us that God is within us: the Holy Spirit in us enables us to call God 'Abba', Father,[15] and when we can't find the words to pray, the Spirit prays within us with 'sighs too deep for words'.[16] So our prayer is to God 'up there', to God 'all around' and to God 'within'. This means that our prayer can be formal and reverent, acknowledging the otherness and holiness of God; our prayer can be earthed, rooted, acknowledging the incarnation of God, that Jesus came to be involved in the life of the world; and our

15. Romans 8:15-16.
16. Romans 8:26.

prayer can be private, intimate, addressing the Spirit who dwells within us. Of course, all our prayer is addressed to the One God, Father, Son and Spirit.

There are two more points here that affect how we pray. Firstly, if the Holy Spirit is constantly praying and interceding within us, then, when we pray, we're not starting something new but, as it were, getting in tune with what's already going on. Our prayer isn't doing something for God but joining in the conversation between Father, Son and Spirit. Secondly, in our prayer we are united with the angels and saints in their prayer in heaven, around the throne of the Lamb.[17]

Prayer and the busy life

The prayer that most of us are best at is asking God for something that we need for ourselves or for someone else. There's nothing wrong with this – it's a recognition of our dependence on God. It can be 'needs-led' – that is, we pray in this way as and when we have a special something to ask of God – or it can be part of our habit of prayer, whereby we regularly pray for what we need. Likewise, our prayer of thanksgiving and praise can be focused or more general, occasional or regular.

If prayer is going to happen for us, we have to create the space for it. This isn't as daunting as it might seem, even in a busy day. Whether it's a few minutes first thing in the morning or some time during a coffee break, any time is good. This is time for 'uncluttered' prayer, a time when we can sit and be more fully aware that we are in the presence of God and can share with God whatever it is that we have to share, and listen to the voice of the Lord. Then there is

---

17. Revelation 7:9-10.

accompanying prayer, where we combine our prayer with whatever else we are doing at the time: it may not be wise to peel potatoes while praying, but it is a great idea to pray whilst peeling potatoes! Space for more reflective prayer might not be available on a daily basis, so then we weave it into our week, at times when the competition for our attention isn't so fierce. And we might possibly find times in the year when we give longer. If we're attentive to our spiritual health, we will find the time!

Praying with others is good, whether at home, church or somewhere else. It is a celebration of the Christ amongst us,[18] and in this context we can find support and encouragement. Again, we can enjoy a mixed diet of spontaneous, extemporary, silent, sung, conversational, meditative and formally composed prayer. Some of our choice here will be influenced by our church tradition, our personality type and who we're praying with. It's all good. The Appendix contains some suggestions about ways to pray with the Bible *(see 'Praying the word of God')*. For now, here are some hints and tips.

You might find it helpful to keep a prayer diary for a while, in which you make a note each day or each week of something about your prayer life. This can help you see how balanced your diet is, and you can decide whether or not you're happy with it. Don't worry about distractions in prayer – they can be useful indicators of what your concerns are at the time, and you can bring them into your prayer; whatever is of interest to you is of interest to the Lord who is interested in you! Look on prayer as a part of who and what you are rather than as a duty to be performed – it's something we owe to God, and something that's life-giving for us. Simplicity is good: God isn't an examiner marking us

18. Matthew 18:20.

on how poetic or wordy we are. Finally, remember it's already going on inside you and in God's presence, and that you are joining in a great hymn to God.

5. The word of the Lord

Leader or another reader: 'And whenever you pray, do not be like the hypocrites; for they love to stand and pray in the synagogues and at the street corners, so that they may be seen by others. Truly I tell you, they have received their reward. But whenever you pray, go into your room and shut the door and pray to your Father who is in secret; and your Father who sees in secret will reward you.

'When you are praying, do not heap up empty phrases as the Gentiles do; for they think that they will be heard because of their many words. Do not be like them, for your Father knows what you need before you ask him.

'Pray then in this way:
Our Father in heaven,
hallowed be your name.
Your kingdom come.
Your will be done,
on earth as it is in heaven.
Give us this day our daily bread.
And forgive us our debts,
as we also have forgiven our debtors.
And do not bring us to the time of trial,
but rescue us from the evil one.
For if you forgive others their trespasses, your heavenly Father will also forgive you; but if you do not forgive others, neither will your Father forgive your trespasses.'
Matthew 6:5-15

6. Reflection

Leader: We know from the Gospels that Jesus prayed frequently to the Father; there were times when he withdrew to a quiet place, away from the crowds; there were times when he prayed in the presence of his disciples; indeed, when they asked him to teach them how to pray, he gave them the great prayer and pattern of prayer, the Our Father. This is a rich text to reflect on, and every word and phrase tells us something: we address God as 'our' Father, the Father of us all; when we say 'Father', we are addressing a God with whom we are in relationship, not an anonymous 'supreme being'. 'Hallowed be your name' indicates our duty of worship and also refers to the holiness, the otherness of God. When we pray 'Your kingdom come, your will be done, on earth as it is in heaven' we are not so much asking God to bring the kingdom, but rather we are aligning ourselves with God's will – may what God wants come about. In asking for our daily bread, we are acknowledging our ongoing dependence on God for our life and well-being. And in asking that we be forgiven 'as we also have forgiven our debtors', we are committing ourselves to be people of forgiveness. This is a prayer not to be prayed lightly! We ask the Father not to bring us to judgement, recognising God's authority to judge and our own unworthiness in God's presence. And we pray to be saved from the evil one, recognising and invoking God's saving power.

In our reflection, we can pray the Our Father and make it our own. We pray it quietly, pondering each word and phrase, exploring what it means to us individually and what it means to our community.

The time of reflection is brought to an end by the leader simply saying, 'Amen'.

7. Talk-talk

- How best do I pray? Have I tried different ways of praying?
- Has the way I pray changed over the years?
- Do I make enough time for prayer?
- What are our main problems with prayer?
- Are there any ways we can help each other in our prayer?
- Do we really believe prayer makes a difference?
- What examples can we give of prayer helping us or someone else?
- What would our ideal 'prayer diet' be?

8. Resolve

Decide whether any practical action needs to be taken as a result of this reflection.

9. Before the Lord

Suggested hymns and songs, if desired:
Jesus, all for Jesus (375)
Lord, I lift my hands to you in prayer (460)
Thy kingdom come! (773)

Leader: 'And this is eternal life, that they may know you, the only true God, and Jesus Christ whom you have sent' (John 17:3).

Leader: In our prayer together, may we come to know God better, and share in the promise of eternal life held out to us. In our prayer together, may we listen to the voice of the Lord in our hearts. In our prayer together, let us ask for all our needs. In our prayer together, may we give thanks. In our prayer together, let us praise the Living God.

Prayer based on Psalm 71[19]

Leader: In you, O Lord, I take refuge;
let me never be put to shame.
All: We look to you, Lord, to guard us and watch over us.
We look to you, Lord, to save us.

Leader: In your righteousness deliver me and rescue me;
incline your ear to me and save me.
All: We look to you, Lord, and to your mercy.
We call on you, confident of your help.

Leader: Be to me a rock of refuge,
a strong fortress, to save me,
for you are my rock and my fortress.
All: We look to you, Lord, our help and our strength.
With you, Lord, we need not fear.

Leader: Rescue me, O my God, from the hand of the wicked,
from the grasp of the unjust and cruel.
All: You are a God of justice, and your judgements are true.
Your way is a way of peace.

Leader: For you, O Lord, are my hope,
my trust, O Lord, from my youth.
All: Lord, when all was lost, you gave us hope.
We live in the hope your promise holds out to us.

19. Psalm 71:1-6.

Leader: Upon you I have leaned from my birth;
it was you who took me from my mother's womb.
My praise is continually of you.
All: You are our God, worthy of all praise.
You alone, Lord, are holy.

Scripture verse

(to be read out loud again, with pause for reflection)

'And this is eternal life, that they may know you, the only true God, and Jesus Christ whom you have sent' (John 17:3).

Leader: Here we can reflect on how we come to know God through prayer, and how prayer nurtures and enriches us.

Petitions

The leader introduces each petition, allowing a pause for silent prayer after each one.

We ask you, Lord, for a spirit of prayer.

We ask you, Lord, for attentiveness to your word.

We ask you, Lord, for healing and wholeness.

We ask you, Lord, to guide us and guard us.

We ask you, Lord, for loving hearts.

Grant us, Lord, a spirit of praise.

Grant us, Lord, your gift of peace.

Grant us, Lord, unity and mutual understanding.

Grant us, Lord, sensitivity to each other's needs.

Grant us, Lord, the intentions we now bring before you . . .

Free prayer may follow.

Thanksgivings

The leader introduces each thanksgiving, allowing a pause for silent prayer after each one.

We thank you, Lord, for your word.

We thank you for this time of sharing.

We thank you, Lord, for our fellowship.

We thank you for the people with whom we share our lives.

We thank you for each new day.

We thank you for the gift of life.

We thank you for all your good gifts, especially . . .

Free prayer may follow.

Our Father . . .

10. Takeaway

A thought and a prayer for each day, which you might find of help, until we meet again *(see Appendix)*.

11. Blessing

All: Father, Creator of all, guard us, guide us and keep us safe. Amen.
Jesus, Saviour, our brother and our friend, stay with us on our journey. Amen.
Spirit of God, blowing freely throughout our world, fill us with courage and strength. Amen.
Father, Son and Spirit, bless us we pray, and bless those whom we love. Amen.

Week five

Giving and not counting the cost: the grateful life

1. Calming down *(pause after each sentence)*

Leader: In this time of prayer, we know the Lord is with us. We are conscious of our surroundings, of each other, of our own bodies and of our breathing. As we breathe, we can imagine ourselves breathing in God and breathing out God; we are immersed in the presence of our loving God.

2. Catching up

Leader: Let us think for a few moments of all that has happened in our lives over the last week: the things we've done, the people we've met, the places we've visited. And we think of what's been on our minds: the worries and cares, the things that have made us smile, the news we want to pass on. We have a chance over the next few minutes to share that with each other – this is the 'me' I have brought here this evening, the 'me' I bring before the Lord.

3. Opening prayer

All: Lord Jesus Christ, our Master and Brother,
in these days of Lent
we recall the forty days you spent in the desert,
preparing to witness to the truth of your Father.
We think of the love you showed us,
what you suffered for us
and the death you endured for us.

And we remember your glorious resurrection from the dead.
Help us always to be mindful of who you are
and all that you have given to us.
Grant that we each may have a grateful heart.
Amen.

4. The matter in hand – the grateful life

According to the playwright Oscar Wilde, a cynic is 'a man who knows the price of everything, and the value of nothing.'[20] This scathing observation is worth examining more closely in relation not just to cynics but to consumerist society. One feature of a consumerist society is the belief that everything has a price, that anything can be bought. Even things that were once regarded as basic rights and should be free are sold for profit. One example is drinking water. In Britain, water is supplied to households and businesses by for-profit water companies; consumers have little choice. The bottled water market has increased dramatically in recent years – now over two billion litres are consumed annually in the UK alone – and has a value of £1.5 billion.[21]

The danger here is that it is so easy to think of everything in terms of purchase rather than gift; to appreciate things not because of their use or beauty or their intrinsic value but because of how much they cost, how much money they are worth. And the other side of this way of viewing the world is that if something is free and does not have a market value, it is not worthy of our attention.

20. The line is spoken by Lord Darlington in *Lady Windermere's Fan*, Act lll.
21. http://www.britishbottledwater.org/vitalstats.html (2012 figures).

Remedy required!

This consumerist view of the world is at odds with our Christian faith. Christians believe that God created all that there is, and that we are stewards of that creation. Christians believe that creation – the whole of creation – was created by God and is 'good'.[22] This affects how we think of our world and everything in it: it is the reason we value and respect other people, it is the reason we believe in true justice and fairness, it is the reason we can appreciate beauty, and it is the reason we give thanks to God. If praise is worshipping God because of who God *is*, thanksgiving is worshipping God because of *what God has done*. A healthy spirituality necessarily includes both elements. We'll come to praise in week 7, so for now our focus is thanksgiving, living the grateful life. There are different aspects to living the grateful life.

Firstly, we have to be aware of what God has given us. This involves reflecting constantly on who we are and what we have; on the people in our lives; on the gift of faith; on the world around us, the air we breathe, the food we eat, the place we live. It means taking nothing for granted.

Secondly, whilst we might look at what we have as earned by our labours, at the people around us as just a random accumulation of people, at the wonders of nature as precisely that – wonders of *nature* – we can also view them as gifts of God, the God who is behind everything, above, within and below everything. This is a way of rightly situating ourselves in creation. It's a way of looking at the world not as something we have a right to, but as a gift.

Thirdly, if we can see all that we have and are as a gift, then we are inevitably led to respond in some way to the

22. Genesis 1:4, 10, 12, 18, 21, 25, 31.

giver. We can see that something is required of us, not due to the demands of our giving God but by our total indebtedness: gratitude is the only appropriate response to the profligate generosity of God. Grateful people count their blessings. However, that's the easy part. Could we, like Job, even give thanks for our trials and tribulations, our deprivations and sufferings? That's probably something we would have to work on! This is the realm of redemption: that God does not insulate us from suffering but is able to bring good out of whatever happens. As Paul says, 'We know that all things work together for good for those who love God, who are called according to his purpose.'[23] If we could really take this on board, we could see God in virtually anything.

Fourthly and finally, gratitude is not an *act*, as such, but an *orientation*; a way of thinking, being and doing, a way of life. So gratitude isn't something we do just when we're feeling churchy or holy; it's something we live all the time. And it's actually a nice way to be. If we were given the choice of spending time with a complainer, someone who constantly moaned about everything and everyone, or spending time with someone who was grateful for everything, full of gratitude, it's not hard to guess which person we would prefer to spend time with. Complainers spread dissatisfaction and unhappiness; grateful people make us more appreciative of what we have and who we are.

The recipe for a grateful life

If we're going to live more gratefully, we need to make a plan, or at least reflect on how we're going to accomplish it. Here are some pointers:

---

23. Romans 8:28.

- Count your blessings, short form. We end the day by recounting everything we have to be grateful for, what has happened during the day, the people we have met. Often this prayer will be routine; sometimes we will give thanks for unexpected blessings. And then we say 'thank you' to God in prayer.
- Count your blessings, long form. This might be something we do at the end of the week, or monthly, or when we find we have time on our hands. We count all our blessings, not just those of the past day. We can thank God for people who are no longer with us, for events in the distant past, or we can simply do a spiritual inventory of everything for which we wish to give thanks.
- Random acts of gratitude. If we suddenly think of a blessing we've received, or something happens that we're glad about, or if the notion of giving thanks happens to come to our mind, then we can give thanks on the spot, there and then. It needn't be an extended thank you; it could be simply, 'Thank you, Lord'. It's like a happy version of swearing!
- Balance your prayer. In week 1 we reflected on the balanced spiritual diet, and we can now use what we've learned: every time we ask for something in prayer, we balance the prayer by giving thanks for something. We train ourselves not just to be askers but to be 'thankers', too.
- Share your blessings. Blessings aren't for hoarding, they're for sharing! If we're grateful to God, we'll want to share that with others. It's a way of brightening someone else's day, and it's much better than grumbling, which changes nothing but celebrates the negative. It's

so much more pleasant to be with someone who's thankful than with someone who's not.

- Look for God in all things. When hard times hit, when our day doesn't go according to plan, when we have to cope with what's unpleasant and undesirable, we can stand back and look for God in the situation. How do we recognise where God is? Well, God will be sharing our suffering; God will be offering comfort; God will be giving wise advice; God will be accepting and forgiving; God will be encouraging; God will be able to see the long term, beyond the present difficulty; God will be giving hope; God will be making good come from the bad; God will be speaking words of peace. If there is anyone around you doing any of these things, what they are doing is from God.
- *Be* a blessing. This isn't quite the same as sharing your blessings; it's doing deeds which make life a little better for others: deeds which help, improve, cheer up, comfort. And it's not really the deeds that are important, rather it's what they say about God, the God who is making you a blessing to others.
- Look after God's gifts. As we've already seen, the grateful person doesn't take God's gifts for granted but recognises them for what they are. The next step is to look after them and not treat them lightly. If the natural world is a gift from God, then we care for it; if other people are a gift, we respect them; if we have talents and abilities, we don't let them rust for lack of use; if we have possessions, we take care of them.
- Stifle a moan! This isn't always easy. But if we consider that every time we moan or grumble we become a little

bit more of a 'moany' person, that should give us the incentive to bite our tongue when we're about to launch into criticism unnecessarily. It's not just that we might be doing someone else harm, but that we also will probably be damaging our own spiritual health.

- Believe in God's providence. We've reflected briefly on redemption, how God can bring good from bad. But we also believe in God's providence, the gentle nudging of the Holy Spirit towards goodness in individuals and in communities. If we believe that God is at work in the world, pushing, tempting, cajoling, luring, wooing us to goodness and holiness, then we see everyday events in a different light: there is a purpose and a power behind it all. And we can be grateful in the most unusual situations.

5. The word of the Lord

Leader or another reader: On the way to Jerusalem Jesus was going through the region between Samaria and Galilee. As he entered a village, ten lepers approached him. Keeping their distance, they called out, saying, 'Jesus, Master, have mercy on us!' When he saw them, he said to them, 'Go and show yourselves to the priests.' And as they went, they were made clean. Then one of them, when he saw that he was healed, turned back, praising God with a loud voice. He prostrated himself at Jesus' feet and thanked him. And he was a Samaritan. Then Jesus asked, 'Were not ten made clean? But the other nine, where are they? Was none of them found to return and give praise to God except this foreigner?' Then he said to him, 'Get up and go on your way; your faith has made you well.'
Luke 17:11-19

Yours, O Lord, are the greatness, the power, the glory, the victory, and the majesty; for all that is in the heavens and on the earth is yours; yours is the kingdom, O Lord, and you are exalted as head above all. Riches and honour come from you, and you rule over all. In your hand are power and might; and it is in your hand to make great and to give strength to all. And now, our God, we give thanks to you and praise your glorious name.
1 Chronicles 29:11-13

6. Reflection

Leader: Jesus worked many miracles of healing, but Luke's account of the cleansing of the ten lepers stands out for several reasons. This was a healing en masse, with a whole group being healed. Secondly, Jesus did not heal the lepers by close contact with them; rather he told them to go to the priests. It was the priests who would have to declare the lepers clean, after which they would be able to be readmitted to the community. But the main point of the story as Luke tells it is twofold: the importance of giving thanks, and the fact that the only one who did so was the foreigner from Samaria. The Samaritan realised that the cure was from God, and that the only appropriate response to such a great gift was thanksgiving. Jesus equates the Samaritan's expression of gratitude with praise of God. It was this recognition of the importance of thanksgiving, this living a life of gratitude, that made the leper clean.

In his letter to the church in Colossae, Paul encourages the community to live a life of thanksgiving, thanking the Father through the Lord Jesus.

The time of reflection is brought to an end by the leader simply saying, 'Amen'.

7. Talk-talk

- Can you name five things for which you are genuinely grateful to God?
- Why do you think the foreigner was the only one to return and thank Jesus?
- Do you think you are a grateful person? Have you ever thought about this before?
- Can you think of a person you know who lives a life of gratitude?
- Is it possible to have a grateful community (such as a church, for example)?
- Is it realistic to give thanks even in hardship?
- 'Eucharist' means 'thanksgiving'. Why is it the name given to the celebration of Holy Communion?

8. Resolve

Decide whether any individual or collective practical action needs to be taken as a result of this prayer and discussion.

9. Before the Lord

Suggested hymns and songs, if desired:
Thanks be to God (696)
Thanks to God whose word was spoken (698)
Now thank we all our God (532)

Leader: 'And whatever you do, in word or deed, do everything in the name of the Lord Jesus, giving thanks to God the Father through him' (Colossians 3:17).

Leader: God is worthy of our thanks and our praise.

Prayer based on Psalm 100

Leader: Make a joyful noise to the Lord, all the earth.
Worship the Lord with gladness;
come into his presence with singing.
All: We give thanks to the Lord.
We bless the Lord.
Together we sing the praises of the Lord!

Leader: Know that the Lord is God.
It is he that made us, and we are his;
we are his people, and the sheep of his pasture.
All: We give thanks to the Lord.
We bless the Lord.
Together we sing the praises of the Lord!

Leader: Enter his gates with thanksgiving,
and his courts with praise.
Give thanks to him, bless his name.
All: We give thanks to the Lord.
We bless the Lord.
Together we sing the praises of the Lord!

Leader: For the Lord is good;
his steadfast love endures for ever,
and his faithfulness to all generations.
All: We give thanks to the Lord.
We bless the Lord.
Together we sing the praises of the Lord!

Scripture verse

(to be read out loud again, with a pause for reflection)

'And whatever you do, in word or deed, do everything in the name of the Lord Jesus, giving thanks to God the Father through him' (Colossians 3:17).

Leader: Here we reflect on the goodness of God.

Petitions

(pause for silent prayer after each)

Leader: For those who do not have what they need to live,
for all whom we know who are sick,
for those who care for the sick,
for this place in which we live,
for the unity of Christians,
for peace in the home, in the community, in our world,
for those who govern us,
we now add our own prayers . . .

Free prayer may now follow.

Thanksgivings

(pause for silent prayer after each)

Leader: For the gift of life,
for the gift of faith,
for those who help us,
for those who encourage us,
for those who love us,
for our daily bread,
for the good news of Jesus Christ,
for our sharing together,
we now add our own thanksgivings . . .

Free prayer may now follow.

Our Father . . .

10. Takeaway

A thought and a prayer for each day, which you might find of help, until we meet again *(see Appendix)*.

11. Blessing

Leader: For the whole of creation,
All: Father, we thank you.

Leader: For our salvation in Christ,
All: Lord Jesus, we thank you.

Leader: For our call to discipleship,
All: Holy Spirit, we thank you.

Leader: May God bless us all,
and bless those whom we love,
now and always.
Amen.

Week six

A helping hand: encouraging each other

1. Calming down *(pause after each sentence)*

Leader: Sitting comfortably, we now relax our bodies, consciously letting go of any physical tension we might be feeling. We relax our minds, letting go of any anxieties and cares for the time being – there'll be time for those later. If distractions intrude, we don't let them worry us. And then we pray that our minds and hearts are open to God's word.

2. Catching up

Leader: Let us think for a few moments of all that has happened in our lives over the last week: the things we've done, the people we've met and the places we've visited. And we think of what's been on our minds: the worries and cares, the things that have made us smile, the news we want to pass on. We have a chance over the next few minutes to share that with each other – this is the 'me' I have brought here this evening, the 'me' I bring before the Lord.

3. Opening prayer

All: Holy Spirit of God,
you have called us together today
that we might reflect on God's word
and allow what we learn to help us grow.
Help us to be aware
of your abiding presence
in our daily lives,

guiding us, inspiring us, prompting us
and encouraging us.
Spirit of the risen Lord,
may we always rejoice
to know you are near.
You who with the Father
and the Son
are One God,
for ever and ever.
Amen.

4. The matter in hand – encouraging each other

The world's first purpose-built hospice for the dying opened in Sydenham, London, in 1967. Previously, people who were terminally ill spent their remaining weeks, months or years in hospitals, nursing homes or institutions run by church organisations. Named St Christopher's, the hospice was the brainchild of Cicely Saunders. Since St Christopher's received its first patients, the hospice movement has spread throughout the world.

Living before dying

Saunders' motto was 'Living before dying', and her aim was to improve the quality of life of those who were terminally ill. She had trained as a nurse but was advised that her ideas for a hospice project would not be listened to unless she was a doctor – and so she studied medicine, qualifying as a doctor in 1957. Saunders had the idea that if she could improve pain control, she could improve the quality of life of the residents: they could spend quality time with family and friends, engage in recreational activities and live as normal a life as possible in the circumstances. She was a pioneer in the field of palliative care: medical treatment not to cure but to improve life. Her obituary in the British Medical Journal stated, 'Saunders introduced the idea of "total pain," which included the physical, emotional, social, and spiritual dimensions of distress. A good listener, she paid systematic attention to patient narratives.'[24] Dame Cicely Saunders died on 14 July 2005 in the hospice she had founded, having radically changed the lives of so many.

Do not be afraid

Saunders' hospice philosophy is holistic; it recognises the variety of issues faced by terminally ill people and offers care across the spectrum of concerns. It is, literally, encouraging – putting new courage into people who might be afraid. It is encouragement in the wider sense, too, giving people new hope and strength. A feature of a healthy spiritual life is the encouragement we can give to others, and our willingness to accept the encouragement of others. Paul in his letters frequently offered encouragement to members of the various churches to which he wrote. The witness of Stephen in The Acts of the Apostles[25] when he was put to death for his faith offered encouragement to the believers, and historically down the centuries Christians have encouraged each other in their following of Christ. And it is part of Christian witness to encourage others, giving hope and new strength. Of course, encouragement is more than just patting someone on the back and telling them, 'You can do it', or 'Well done'.

If we want to be encouragers, we have to work on it. It will help us to be spiritually fit, and will help other people too.

---

24. http://www.bmj.com/content/331/7510/238.
25. Acts 6:8–7:60.

We're going to look at five aspects of encouraging, all related and all necessary: accompanying, listening, empathising, affirming and enabling.

Accompanying

It sounds obvious, but it needs saying anyway: to encourage someone we have to spend some time with them. Just as the Lord walked with the disciples on the Emmaus road, we can spend time with each other. It doesn't matter so much what we are doing; it's our presence that's important. Our presence is a sharing of the life of the person we're with; it familiarises us with their circumstances, how they are, what they might need. Spending time with someone is a way of saying that they are of value, worth spending time with; this in itself is an encouragement. Many people suffer from low self-esteem; they see themselves as of little value, and this holds them back in life. They feel that others are better, more gifted, more deserving, and they don't like to ask for help in case the answer is 'no'. So our response is to be there for them, literally, accompanying them on their journey. Of course, it's not just the amount of time we spend with them that counts, but we'll come on to that shortly.

Listening

It has been said that for most people the opposite of speaking isn't listening; it's waiting. This is when we're not really hearing what someone else is saying, we're just waiting for a gap in the conversation so we can speak our part. This isn't good enough for us. When we're with someone, a friend, colleague, or anyone else, it's good to listen to them and to hear what they are saying, in terms of the words they use, how they use them, and the tone with which they speak.

When we hear well, we can respond well. When we don't listen, the chances are that our response will be off the mark in some way. So really listening when we're in conversation means it's more likely to be a good conversation.

Listening is encouraging too. When we say that we've managed to 'get something off our chest', we usually mean that we've spoken about it to someone who really listened. And if they listened well, we feel as though we have been heard, and that's vital.

One more feature of good listening is that it's not primarily *passive* – that is, we don't just sit still and say nothing. Real listening is *active* – we nod, agree, ask questions, gently prompt. In short, we encourage the person to speak, and in doing so give encouragement to them.

Empathising

Sympathy is seeing the suffering of someone and feeling sorry for them. We don't necessarily know how they feel but we, as it were, read their distress signals and are moved. 'Compassion' is a related word. In the Gospels, we hear a number of times how Jesus was 'moved with compassion'. This doesn't merely mean he felt sorry for people, or showed pity. It means that seeing their suffering, he (literally) suffered with them, and this prompted him, usually, to perform a miracle of healing.

Somewhere between these two is empathy. This is where we feel the suffering of someone else, actually suffering with him or her and identifying with what they are going through in a real way. But we don't necessarily feel prompted to do anything other than to be with the one who is suffering. Mary standing by the cross of Jesus suffered with her Son, as any mother would surely share the suffering of her child.

Sometimes we can feel the suffering of others, and even though we may be able to do little to alleviate their suffering, we can offer solidarity. So while we are accompanying, say, our friend, we listen to them. Hearing how they feel, we try to empathise, to enter their suffering with them; we're in emotional solidarity with them, and they're not alone. It's so encouraging when someone empathises with us, and empathy is a gift we can share with others.

Affirming

The baptism of Jesus by John in the Jordan river was accompanied, according to the Gospel accounts, by high drama: as Jesus was baptised, he saw the heavens split apart and the Spirit descending on him like a dove, and a voice came from heaven saying, 'You are my Son, the Beloved; with you I am well pleased.'[26] The voice of the Father was affirming Jesus, and there can be no greater affirmation than that which comes from God.

Time and again in his ministry, Jesus affirmed those who did not imagine themselves as having any worth. Affirmation is recognising what is good and naming it as good. When people do not fully believe in themselves, or imagine that they have nothing to offer, affirming who they are and the gifts they have (but which they might not recognise) can be a tremendous encouragement to them.

The opposite of affirmation is envy, which desires the destruction of what is good because it is good. We see something that is good and, because it is not ours – because it belongs to someone else – we wish to spoil it (jealousy is different – it's where we simply want whatever it is for our-

26. Mark 1:9-11.

selves). Affirmation, on the other hand, is naming goodness and celebrating it, encouraging the person who is affirmed.

Enabling

The final ingredient in encouragement is enabling people to do what they might not otherwise be able to do. When Jesus breathed the Holy Spirit onto the disciples at Pentecost, he transformed fearful, cowering individuals into a courageous community, into people who were eager and emboldened to preach the good news. He enabled them. We can enable people by assisting them, resourcing them, inspiring them and helping them to believe in themselves. The final piece of our encouragement jigsaw is now in place!

5. The word of the Lord

Leader or another reader: John the baptiser appeared in the wilderness, proclaiming a baptism of repentance for the forgiveness of sins. And people from the whole Judean countryside and all the people of Jerusalem were going out to him, and were baptised by him in the river Jordan, confessing their sins. Now John was clothed with camel's hair, with a leather belt around his waist, and he ate locusts and wild honey. He proclaimed, 'The one who is more powerful than I is coming after me; I am not worthy to stoop down and untie the thong of his sandals. I have baptised you with water; but he will baptise you with the Holy Spirit.'

In those days Jesus came from Nazareth of Galilee and was baptised by John in the Jordan. And just as he was coming up out of the water, he saw the heavens torn apart and the Spirit descending like a dove on him. And a voice came from heaven, 'You are my Son, the Beloved; with you I am well pleased.'

And the Spirit immediately drove him out into the wilderness. He was in the wilderness for forty days, tempted by Satan; and he was with the wild beasts; and the angels waited on him.
Mark 1:4-13

He entered Jericho and was passing through it. A man was there named Zacchaeus; he was a chief tax-collector and was rich. He was trying to see who Jesus was, but on account of the crowd he could not, because he was short in stature. So he ran ahead and climbed a sycomore tree to see him, because he was going to pass that way. When Jesus came to the place, he looked up and said to him, 'Zacchaeus, hurry and come down; for I must stay at your house today.' So he hurried down and was happy to welcome him. All who saw it began to grumble and said, 'He has gone to be the guest of one who is a sinner.' Zacchaeus stood there and said to the Lord, 'Look, half of my possessions, Lord, I will give to the poor; and if I have defrauded anyone of anything, I will pay back four times as much.' Then Jesus said to him, 'Today salvation has come to this house, because he too is a son of Abraham. For the Son of Man came to seek out and to save the lost.'
Luke 19:1-10

6. Reflection

Leader: The context of the baptism of Jesus is important. John the Baptist gives testimony to how important Jesus is, preparing us for the ultimate affirmation when it is made by the Father. After his baptism, Jesus is driven into the wilderness to be tested – strengthened by the knowledge that he is the Beloved of the Father. So the affirmation is a confirmation of the truth of who Jesus is. In Matthew's account of the Transfiguration of Jesus, the Father's voice says, 'This is my Son, the Beloved; with him I am well pleased; listen to him!'[27] Here the Father's affirmation has consequences for Peter, James and John who witness the event: they are to pay attention to the words of Jesus.

As a fraudulent tax-collector, Zacchaeus is clearly not a popular person. He might not fare too well if he were to mingle with the crowds whom he has cheated. In his encounter with Jesus, the Lord doesn't judge Zacchaeus, or even forgive him; he simply accepts him, sees beyond his wrongdoing and affirms his humanity. For Zacchaeus, this affirmation is life changing. He has been saved. In our reflection, let us imagine the Lord speaking to us, looking beyond anything wrong we have done, beyond our failures, and seeing the goodness and the love. In this way we are affirmed, as only God can affirm us.

The time of reflection is brought to an end by the leader simply saying, 'Amen'.

7. Talk-talk

- Can we think of people who have encouraged us? How did they do it?
- Are there people we ourselves have encouraged? Did it make a difference?
- What difference has encouragement made to our lives?
- In our community, do we encourage each other?
- Practically speaking, how could we encourage each other more?
- Do we feel that God encourages us? If so, how?

27. Matthew 17:5.

8. Resolve

Decide whether any practical action needs to be taken as a result of this reflection.

9. Before the Lord

Suggested hymns and songs, if desired:
Father welcomes all his children (179)
Zacchaeus was a very little man (857)
Lord of all hopefulness (467)

Leader: 'May the God of steadfastness and encouragement grant you to live in harmony with one another, in accordance with Christ Jesus, so that together you may with one voice glorify the God and Father of our Lord Jesus Christ.' (Romans 15:5, 6)

Prayer based on Psalm 23

Leader: The Lord is my shepherd, I shall not want.
He makes me lie down in green pastures;
All: The Lord is our shepherd.
With the Lord we will lack nothing.

Leader: he leads me beside still waters;
he restores my soul.
All: With the Lord is refreshment.
With the Lord is peace.

Leader: He leads me in right paths
for his name's sake.
All: Should we stray, the Lord will seek us.
The Lord will find us and lead us home.

Leader: Even though I walk through the darkest valley,
I fear no evil;

All: The Lord's presence encourages us.
The Lord's presence strengthens us.

Leader: for you are with me;
your rod and your staff –
they comfort me.
All: Truly the Lord is our shepherd.
The Lord is with us.

Leader: You prepare a table before me
in the presence of my enemies;
All: With the Lord there is abundance.
With the Lord we are truly blessed.

Leader: you anoint my head with oil;
my cup overflows.
All: The Lord has made us a holy people.
The generosity of the Lord knows no bounds.

Leader: Surely goodness and mercy shall follow me
all the days of my life,
All: Our life with the Lord brings blessings.
The Lord is with us always.

Leader: and I shall dwell in the house of the Lord
my whole life long.
All: The promise of eternal life is given to us.
The promises of the Lord are sure.

Scripture verse

(to be read out loud again, with a pause for reflection)

'May the God of steadfastness and encouragement grant you to live in harmony with one another, in accordance with Christ Jesus, so that together you may with one voice glorify the God and Father of our Lord Jesus Christ' (Romans 15:5, 6).

Leader: Paul describes God as the 'God of steadfastness and encouragement'. Here we reflect on how God encourages us, and how we can encourage each other.

Petitions

(to be read by the leader or another reader)

Pause after each petition for free prayer, then say together,
'In your goodness, Lord, help us.'
That we may be gentle with the discouraged,
that we may be accompaniers,
that we may be listeners,
that we may be empathisers,
that we may be affirmers,
that we may be enablers,
that we may be encouragers . . .

Free prayer may now follow.

Thanksgivings

Pause after each thanksgiving then say together,
'In all things, Lord we thank you'
for those who have helped us,
for those who have accompanied us,
for those who have listened to us,
for those who have empathised with us,
for those who have affirmed us,
for those who have enabled us,
for those who have encouraged us . . .

Free prayer may now follow.

Our Father . . .

10. Takeaway

A thought and a prayer for each day, which you might find of help, until we meet again *(see Appendix).*

11. Blessing

Leader: God is the Lord of the whole of creation.
All: Blessed be God.

Leader: God is almighty and everlasting.
All: Blessed be God.

Leader: God is compassion and love.
All: Blessed be God.

Pause

All: May God bless us,
our families and friends
this day and always.
Amen.

Week seven

Fit for a king: being a people of praise

1. Calming down *(pause after each sentence)*

Leader: Knowing that we are in the presence of our risen Lord, let us be still. The voice of the Holy Spirit within us is a voice that speaks words of peace, a peace that only God can give. Let us be calm, resting in God's peace.

2. Catching up

Leader: Let us think for a few moments of all that has happened in our lives over the last week: the things we've done, the people we've met, the places we've visited. And we think of what's been on our minds: the worries and cares, the things that have made us smile, the news we want to pass on. We have a chance over the next few minutes to share that with each other – this is the 'me' I have brought here this evening, the 'me' I bring before the Lord.

3. Opening prayer

All: Loving Father,
you raised your Son, Jesus Christ,
from the dead.
He who gave his life for us is alive
and can die no more.
As his sacrifice gave glory to you,
and as you have glorified him,
let us give you thanks
and fill our hearts with praise.

Through Jesus Christ our risen Lord,
in the Holy Spirit.
Amen.

4. The matter in hand – being a people of praise

On 10 December every year the Nobel Peace Prize, the world's most prestigious prize for furthering the cause of peace, is awarded. The Nobel laureate is chosen by the Nobel Committee and special advisors who each year share the task of choosing the individual – or the people – who are to receive the prize. Other Nobel awards, for achievements in the fields of science and literature, are generally made years after the achievement being recognised, so its significance may be seen to have stood the test of time. The Peace Prize, however, usually has more of a contemporary reference, in the hope that the award will stimulate the promotion of peace by the winner and by others. The Nobel Prize ceremony, in common with all such occasions, has at its heart the Citation – a recounting of what the winner has done and achieved and the difference it has made. Because the peace award is sometimes controversial, the Citation is very important indeed, and studied closely. The Citation is read out and the winner/s (or someone representing them) receive the diploma, a medal, and a monetary prize.

Recounting what God has done and who God is

We made the distinction in week 5 between thanksgiving as worshipping God because of *what God has done* and praise being the worship of God because of *who God is*. Whilst this is true, in practice it's difficult to separate the two, as we come to know who God is by reflecting on God's deeds, and infer God's nature from God's actions. In both cases, the focus is on God.

When we praise God we, in effect, include a citation that describes why we are doing so. It either gives attributes to God such as 'Loving', 'Almighty' or 'Saviour', or it recalls the acts of God on our behalf: 'You who created heaven and earth', 'O God, you sent your Son Jesus to save us' or 'Holy Spirit, you give us the courage to spread the good news'. At times we do both, of course. Our citation may focus on what God has done in the past, on what God is doing now and on what we learn about God from that. These are the mind and heart aspects of praise, the parts we're most aware of. But our spirit reaches out to God in praise too, the Holy Spirit praying within us and prompting us to pray. Real praise is when we are worshipping God with every part of our being. The vision of John in Revelation of the saints worshipping before the throne of God is a rich evocation of praise. We'll reflect on this later.

Doing what we are created to do

When asked what was the greatest commandment of the law, Jesus replied, 'You shall love the Lord your God with all your heart, and with all your soul, and with all your mind.'[28] This echoing of the words in Deuteronomy[29] suggests that this fully involved and fully committed love of God is the central purpose of our lives. With our wholehearted love of God belongs the duty and privilege of praise: this is our response to the all-holy God, the God who created heaven and earth, who sent Jesus to save us and the Holy Spirit to inspire us. Our praise must be as perfect as our love, something we do

28. Matthew 22:37.
29. Deuteronomy 6:5.

with our hearts, our souls, our minds and our strength, something which is not just a prayer but, as we mentioned in week 5 in relation to gratitude, is a whole orientation of our life, permeating everything we think, say and do. We can say therefore that we are created to give praise to God, and when we are giving God glory and praise, we truly are 'fit for purpose'. Praise is the fitting response to *who God is.*

Lifted out of our selves

Looking at the same four walls and ceiling all day long affects us; if we don't go outside we begin to forget that there is a world on the other side of our front door. All our problems, anxieties and fears magnify when we are locked in with them and have nothing to distract us. We can feel, in some conscious or unconscious way, trapped.

Imagine for a moment that the world was permanently covered by cloud. Forget the scientific problems this would cause – we're in the realm of imagination. Our earth would begin to seem to be a very small place, self-contained, with no points of reference outside itself. We would know night and day but we wouldn't actually be able to see the sun, moon and stars. This suggests what our spirit would be like without praise, which draws us out of ourselves, beyond ourselves, beyond what we can perceive with our senses, and into the realm of God. The literal meaning of 'ecstasy' is 'standing outside' ourselves, and this is what praise involves. That isn't to say we will have 'out of body' experiences or live in some kind of mystical world all the time, but it does mean that in praise we are being drawn towards and into God in a spiritual way. Obviously we don't need to think of this all the time – if we did, we'd be busy looking for spiritual symptoms every time we give praise to God! But it's good to have an awareness that in prayer, and in praise particularly, we are on holy ground.[30]

Charles Wesley's evocative hymn 'Love divine, all loves excelling' is a rich blend of petitionary prayer. It is a celebration of what God has done and is doing, a celebration of who God is and an anticipation of the restoration of all things in Christ as prophesied by John in the book of Revelation. Wesley looks forward to the completion of God's new creation, to God's people being made 'pure and spotless', taking their place in heaven and ultimately being 'lost in wonder, love and praise'. Wesley knew that to contemplate being lost in wonder, love and praise in this way would be truly inspirational, and to aim for this would be truly a noble aim.

Alleluia – the Easter song

The word 'Alleluia' (or Hallelujah) appears a number of times in the Psalms and means 'Praise God'. It doesn't crop up in the Bible again until Revelation, where it occurs several times, with a similar meaning. Since the time of the early Church theologians, however, Alleluia has been an Easter word, used in liturgy and prayer in praise of the risen Christ. After the resurrection, everything changed: we now pray to the Father in the Holy Spirit, through the risen Christ, and our hymn of praise always has an 'Alleluia' ring to it. Even in deepest, darkest Lent, and in Holy Week as the story of Jesus' suffering and death are solemnly recalled, the Lord is still risen. The Alleluia in Lent might be muted, but it never really goes away. Now, in the bright light of Easter, we can sing our Alleluia with full voice: the Lord is truly risen, he is risen indeed.

30. Like Moses was, as described in Exodus 3:5.

5. The word of the Lord

Leader or another reader: As he approached Jericho, a blind man was sitting by the roadside begging. When he heard a crowd going by, he asked what was happening. They told him, 'Jesus of Nazareth is passing by.' Then he shouted, 'Jesus, Son of David, have mercy on me!' Those who were in front sternly ordered him to be quiet; but he shouted even more loudly, 'Son of David, have mercy on me!' Jesus stood still and ordered the man to be brought to him; and when he came near, he asked him, 'What do you want me to do for you?' He said, 'Lord, let me see again.' Jesus said to him, 'Receive your sight; your faith has saved you.' Immediately he regained his sight and followed him, glorifying God; and all the people, when they saw it, praised God.
Luke 18:35-43

And from the throne came a voice saying,
'Praise our God, all you his servants,
and all who fear him, small and great.'
Then I heard what seemed to be the voice of a great multitude, like the sound of many waters and like the sound of mighty thunder-peals, crying out, 'Hallelujah! For the Lord our God the Almighty reigns. Let us rejoice and exult and give him the glory, for the marriage of the Lamb has come, and his bride has made herself ready; to her it has been granted to be clothed with fine linen, bright and pure' – for the fine linen is the righteous deeds of the saints. And the angel said to me, 'Write this: Blessed are those who are invited to the marriage supper of the Lamb.'
Revelation 19:5-9

6. Reflection

Leader: Notice the emotional narrative in the Gospel account of the cure of the blind man of Jericho. The man is curious and asks who is passing by; he expresses his desperate need for mercy; he is determined to attract the attention of Jesus; he trusts Jesus, asking to be cured; he is cured and glorifies God; his praise is infectious and the whole crowd gives praise to God. A story that begins with desperate need ends in praise – a pattern that recurs again and again in the Gospels. This same pattern occurs in our own lives too: we trust and believe that God can use all things for good, and what begins with desperation can, by God's mercy and grace, end in praise.

John's vision in Revelation is like a glimpse into the spiritual future, when all will be made new. We can keep this image before us to inspire us and encourage us and prompt us to give praise to God. In our time of reflection now, we can ask God for a spirit of praise, to be able to praise God at all times.

The time of reflection is brought to an end by the leader simply saying, 'Amen'.

7. Talk-talk

- Is praising God a significant part of your prayer life?
- How essential do you think that praising God is for a healthy spiritual life?
- Have there been times when you have found that praise comes naturally and easily?
- What kind of prayer (e.g. petition, thanksgiving, praise) do you find most challenging?

- Does your community give adequate attention to the praise of God?
- Is faith chiefly about how we live now, what we believe, our relationship with God, spiritual insurance . . . or what?

8. Resolve

Decide whether any practical action needs to be taken as a result of this reflection.

9. Before the Lord

Suggested hymns and songs, if desired:
Alleluia, alleluia, give thanks to the risen Lord (31)
Christ the Lord is risen again (102)
O worship the King (582)
Love divine, all loves excelling (491)

Leader: 'Through [Jesus], then, let us continually offer a sacrifice of praise to God, that is, the fruit of lips that confess his name' (Hebrews 13:15).

Prayer based on Psalm 150

Leader: Praise the Lord!
Praise God in his sanctuary;
All: Let everything that breathes praise the Lord!

Leader: praise him in his mighty firmament!
Praise him for his mighty deeds;
All: Let everything that breathes praise the Lord!

Leader: praise him according to his surpassing greatness!
Praise him with trumpet sound;
All: Let everything that breathes praise the Lord!

Leader: praise him with lute and harp!
Praise him with tambourine and dance;
All: Let everything that breathes praise the Lord!

Leader: praise him with strings and pipe!
Praise him with clanging cymbals;
All: Let everything that breathes praise the Lord!

Leader: praise him with loud clashing cymbals!
Let everything that breathes praise the Lord!
All: Let everything that breathes praise the Lord!

Leader: Praise the Lord!

Scripture verse

(to be read out loud again, with a pause for reflection)

Leader: 'Through [Jesus], then, let us continually offer a sacrifice of praise to God, that is, the fruit of lips that confess his name' (Hebrews 13:15).

Leader: The author of the letter to the Hebrews urges us to offer a *continual* sacrifice of praise to God – praise not just for the moment but throughout our lives. Let us reflect on what this means for us.

Petitions

(to be read by the leader or another reader)

Pause after each petition, then say together,
'We call on you, Lord, confident of your unfailing help.'

For peace between nations,
for respect between faiths,
for harmony in our community,
for those searching for God,
for people living in sadness and fear,

for new hope,
for the courage to witness,
for those whom we know in need of healing,
for all our needs,
for resurrection joy . . .

Free prayer may now follow.

Praises

(to be read by the leader or another reader)

Pause after each prayer of praise, then say together,
'Lord, we praise and bless you.'

You, O God, are eternal.
You, whose name is mercy,
you, who are compassion and love.
God before all the ages,
God who made heaven and earth,
God, whom we dare to call Father,
you sent your Son to save us.
You raised your Son from death.
In your Son you make all things new . . .

Free prayer may now follow.

Our Father . . .

10. Takeaway

A thought and a prayer for each day, which you might find of help, until we meet again *(see Appendix).*

11. Blessing

Leader: God is good and worthy of all our praise. We ask God to bless us now and to keep alive in us the joy of the risen Christ.

All: May God go before us,
may God be behind us,
and may God surround us.
May God's love enfold us,
may God's strength protect us,
and may God bless us,
Father, Son and Spirit.
Amen.

Appendix

Takeaway

A thought and a prayer for each day from Ash Wednesday to Easter Sunday. These may be printed out and distributed each week to each member of the group.

Week 1

We are what we eat: a healthy spiritual diet

1. Prayer nourishes the spirit.
2. *Heavenly Father, help me to pray.*
3. God's Spirit is praying within me.
4. *Spirit of God, help me to be aware of your presence.*
5. Eat to live, pray to thrive.
6. *Lord, help me to grow in spirit.*
7. I have been entrusted with God's word.
8. *Help me, O God, to ponder your word.*

Week 2

Exercising the heart: loving and living

1. God is love.
2. *Lord Jesus, help me to live in your love.*
3. Jesus came to bring fullness of life.
4. *Help me, Lord, to live fully in your presence.*
5. If we look in the mirror, do we see a loving person?
6. *Lord, help me to love.*
7. Where and with whom have I failed in loving?
8. *Lord, grant me your forgiveness and peace.*
9. Love can make us do great things.
10. *Father, help me to show love in everything I say and do.*

11. Am I affected when I see the needs of others?
12. *Jesus, let me share your compassion and love.*
13. The glory of God is the human person fully alive.
14. *May my life give glory to you, O God.*

Week 3

Losing the baggage: letting go of what's weighing us down

1. Imagine if we were charged for all the 'baggage' we carry around. . .
2. *Lord, help me to let go of bitterness and resentments.*
3. Not showing forgiveness hurts both ways.
4. *O God of mercy, help me to forgive as I am forgiven.*
5. Love drives out fear.
6. *Show me how to love, Lord, so I need not fear.*
7. Love is blind.
8. *Take away any prejudice that is in me, Lord Jesus.*
9. A problem shared is a problem halved.
10. *When I see a neighbour's need, inspire me to help, Spirit of God.*
11. The truth will set you free.
12. *Holy Spirit, lead me into all truth.*
13. Treat others as you would have them treat you.
14. *Help me to be kind, patient, gentle and just, Lord God.*

Week 4

Onwards and upwards: living prayerfully

1. Prayer can move mountains.
2. *Lord, help me to pray.*
3. Do not babble like the pagans do.
4. *May I pray simply and directly, O God.*
5. Pray unceasingly.

6. *Help me, O Lord, to live a prayerful life.*
7. I keep my feet firmly on the ground.
8. *May my prayer be real, Lord.*
9. I look upwards to the stars.
10. *May my prayer be focused on you, Lord God.*
11. As I nourish my body, I must nourish my spirit too.
12. *Father, give me, I pray, my daily bread.*
13. God alone is worthy of worship.
14. *Help me to worship you alone, O Holy Trinity.*

Week 5

Giving and not counting the cost: the grateful life

1. Have I complained more than I've thanked recently?
2. *Help me, Lord, to appreciate all I have.*
3. Blessings are for sharing.
4. *May I be as generous to others as you are to me, O God.*
5. What we take for granted, we cannot fully enjoy.
6. *Lord Jesus, help me to count my blessings and give thanks.*
7. God is in all situations.
8. *Help me as I try to find you in my life, O Lord.*
9. All things work together for good for those who love God.
10. *I give you thanks, Lord, for your Providence.*
11. There are people in my life who are gifts to me.
12. *Let me take none of your gifts for granted, Lord.*
13. I would like to be a blessing in the lives of those I meet.
14. *Help me to be more like you, Lord Jesus.*

Week 6

A helping hand: encouraging each other

1. The Holy Spirit filled the disciples with courage.
2. *Holy Spirit of God, give me courage.*

3. My life would be poorer without the encouragement of others.
4. *Help me, O God, to encourage those with whom I share my life.*
5. Jesus affirmed people, and changed lives.
6. *Help me to recognise what is good, Lord, and to affirm it.*
7. It's good to talk.
8. *Let me be a listening ear to those who need me.*
9. Jesus walked with the disciples on the Emmaus road.
10. *May I accompany those who are lonely.*
11. Jesus was moved by human suffering.
12. *Holy Spirit, make me sensitive to those in pain.*
13. God gives a peace the world cannot give.
14. *Holy Spirit of God, grant me your peace.*

Week 7

Fit for a king: being a people of praise

1. As Jesus entered Jerusalem, the people shouted, 'Hosanna'.
2. *May I greet you as my King, Lord Jesus.*
3. God redeems and makes good.
4. *Help me to trust in your saving power, Lord.*
5. Jesus forgave Peter when he denied him.
6. *Forgive me, Lord, when I fail.*
7. Jesus commanded his disciples to love one another.
8. *May people know we are Christians by the way we love.*
9. Jesus showed us the supreme example of love, dying for us.
10. *As we share in your death, Lord Jesus, may we share your risen life.*
11. The empty tomb is a sign of hope.
12. *Your resurrection, Lord, brings joy to the whole world.*
13. The disciples rejoiced at the presence of their risen Lord.
14. *You are alive, Lord Jesus, and I praise you.*

Spiritual diet sheet: questions to help us reflect on the balance in our spiritual life

These questions can be adapted for group use. There are no right or wrong answers here.

1. Scriptures

- Do I regularly read or listen to the word of God in the Bible? Is this often enough?
- Do I use the word of God in my prayers?
- Is how I live influenced by the word of God?
- Do I share the word of God with others?
- Do I study the word of God in order to understand it more fully?

2. Prayer

- Do I pray every day?
- Am I stuck in a rut with prayer?
- Do I vary the way I pray?
- Do I balance asking, thanking and praising in my prayer?
- Do I pray for long enough?
- Is my prayer adapted to my state in life (e.g. parent, retired, student, etc)?
- Can I think of ways of improving my prayer life?
- Have I spoken with anyone else about prayer?

3. Other spiritual nourishment

- Does my reading nourish me?
- Does beauty inspire me to pray?
- Does suffering prompt me to pray?
- What else prompts me to pray?
- Do the people around me help me in my spiritual life?
- Is my church the right one for me?

4. What I believe

- Am I sufficiently clear about what I believe, in faith terms?
- Do I need to know more?
- Have I ever helped anyone else to faith?
- Is my faith mainly doctrinal, practical, value-led, intuitive, social?
- How important is my faith to me?
- Do I really believe in God? in the resurrection? in heaven? in hell?

5. Worship

- Do I attend church often enough? at all? Does it bother me when I don't attend?
- Is my preferred church evangelical? charismatic? community-based? 'high church'? a particular denomination?
- Am I introvert or extrovert in my worship preferences?
- I chose my present church because of the preaching? community? location? worship style? music ministry? belief statement? social activism? particular ministry? other reason?
- What, if anything, would cause me to change church?
- Would I recommend my church to others?
- What is best and worst about my church?

6. Evangelism

- Am I keen to share my faith with others? Or shy?
- What would be the thing I would most want to share?
- Am I doing enough to introduce others to Jesus and my faith?
- What could I do that I am not doing?
- Do I feel called to share my faith?
- Which Christian do I most admire? Why?

Praying the word of God

Some suggestions for pondering the Scriptures

In each case, begin with a prayer asking God to open up the word for you, by the power of the Holy Spirit.

Pray a word or a phrase

- Read a passage of Scripture slowly and reflectively until a word or phrase strikes you. Pause. Turn over the word or phrase repeatedly in your mind. Bring it into a prayer.

Praying the narrative

- If the Scripture passage is a story from one of the Gospels (or from the Old Testament), read it slowly and reflectively. Note the narrative: what happens, what happens next, and so on. Then notice any spiritual narrative: for example, in a healing miracle there might be human need, a cry for help, the miracle of healing, gratitude and praise. Finally, notice the emotional narrative: in the same healing miracle there could be desperation, expectation, amazement and joy. Bring what you have noticed into prayer.

Praying values and themes

- Similarly, when reading a passage of Scripture, note what *values* are present, both positive and negative: for example, compassion, love, forgiveness, encouragement, hypocrisy, selfishness, betrayal. Pray for the positive values, and that you be 'led not into temptation'.[31] This exercise may be varied by looking for *themes*, rather than values.

---

31. See Matthew 6:13.

Contemplating the word

- Sit with a passage of Scripture and read it through. Turn the whole passage over and over in your mind gently, not struggling to understand it fully but allowing God to give you some spiritual insight from it. Close with prayer.

Studying and praying

- Study the Scripture with a commentary, one that's neither too simplistic nor too academic. You're looking not so much for *knowledge* here as for *insight*. Again, finish with prayer.

Imagination and prayer

- If the genre of the Scripture is suitable (for example, a Gospel or an Old Testament story, or a narrative passage from Acts) read the passage through two or three times, noticing all the details. Now read it slowly again, imagining that you are in the scene yourself. Bring the experience into your prayer.

Feelings and prayer

- Read a passage from the Scriptures slowly, then read it again. As you read it the second time, be aware of how you *feel* while you are reading, and after you have finished. Does your reading make you feel any emotion? Does it leave you indifferent? Does how you feel surprise you? Bring it all into prayer.

Spiritual fitness quiz

A light-hearted assessment of our spiritual health. Just for fun!

1. **I get up on Sunday morning and it's raining.**
   a. I go back to bed.
   b. I say a prayer and go back to bed.
   c. I head out to church – whether it's hail, rain or shine.

2. **I start to read the Bible from beginning to end.**
   a. I give up in the middle of Leviticus.
   b. OK, it's slow going at times, but I make it to Revelation.
   c. I miss out all the heavy bits but read the rest.

3. **I hear something in a sermon I think is unsound.**
   a. I don't worry – we all make mistakes.
   b. I interrupt the preacher.
   c. I have a conversation with the preacher after church.

4. **A friend has lent me a spiritual book and asks for it back (I haven't read it).**
   a. I confess to not reading it but ask for it again, intending to read it.
   b. I pretend I've read it.
   c. I confess that I never read spiritual books.

5. **I accidentally walk out of a shop with something I haven't paid for.**
   a. I return the item as soon as possible.
   b. I intend to return it but never quite get round to it.
   c. I keep the item and blame the security guard for not stopping me.

6. **A really boring person has asked to talk something over with me.**
   a. I agree to chat but keep putting it off.
   b. I make time and have the chat.
   c. I make excuses and recommend someone else.

7. **My friend made me a cake. I hate cake and gave it away.**
   a. I said I gave it away to a hungry person (I didn't!).
   b. I told her what I did and why.
   c. I pretended I ate and enjoyed it.

8. **In the Holy Trinity**
   a. There are three Gods in one person.
   b. There are three persons in one God.
   c. I don't have a clue!

9. **At the Last Supper, Jesus told his disciples to break bread and drink wine in his memory.**
   a. He just said, 'As often as you do this . . .'
   b. Every Sunday.
   c. Not sure.

10. **The greatest commandment, according to Jesus, is**
   a. Do not eat the fruit from the Tree of Knowledge.
   b. Love your neighbour as yourself.
   c. Love the Lord your God with all your heart, soul and mind.

11. Who announced to Mary that she was to bear God's Son?

a. The archangel Raphael.
b. The shepherds in the field.
c. The archangel Gabriel.

12. What is the meaning of the word 'angel'?

a. A very good person.
b. Someone with wings.
c. Messenger.

13. An evangelist is someone

a. Who spreads the gospel.
b. Who wrote books a long time ago.
c. A kind of angel.

14. To be a Christian, you have to

a. Believe in Jesus Christ.
b. Be a nice person.
c. Neither of the above.

15. You hold a grudge against someone. Is it better to

a. Go to church first, then if you feel better, forgive them?
b. Try to forgive them before you go to church?
c. There's nothing wrong with holding on to a grudge!

16. There's a rainbow in the sky

a. That's a sign of good luck!
b. It reminds you of Moses in the Bible.
c. You think of Noah and the ark.

17. **You're late for work and you spot an older person lying on the pavement in front of you. You . . .**
    a. Anonymously dial social services for help.
    b. Cross the road – it's not your problem.
    c. Stop and see what's wrong, and what you can do to help.

18. **Your minister/pastor/priest is a gossip.**
    a. You tell him/her gently they should know better.
    b. You listen and learn!
    c. You use him/her to your advantage.

19. **Your minister/pastor/priest has power issues and likes to control, so . . .**
    a. You let him/her have their way.
    b. You organise resistance.
    c. You tackle him/her in the light of the gospel.

20. **The bones of Jesus are allegedly found. You . . .**
    a. Are not affected in any way – your experience tells you he's alive.
    b. Will not let any evidence, no matter how scientifically convincing, affect your faith.
    c. Give a sigh of relief and say 'I always knew it was a long shot.'

Here's the scoring (you might disagree – that's ok, this is just for fun, and it just might provoke discussion!)

1. a = 1, b = 2, c = 3
2. a = 1, b = 3, c = 2
3. a = 2, b = 1, c = 3
4. a = 3, b = 1, c = 2

5. a = 3, b = 2, c = 1
6. a = 2, b = 3, c = 1
7. a = 1, b = 3, c = 2
8. a = 1, b = 3, c = 2
9. a = 3, b = 1, c = 2
10. a = 1, b = 2, c = 3
11. a = 2, b = 1, c = 3
12. a = 2, b = 1, c = 3
13. a = 3, b = 2, c = 1
14. a = 3, b = 2, c = 1
15. a = 2, b = 3, c = 1
16. a = 1, b = 2, c = 3
17. a = 2, b = 1, c = 3
18. a = 3, b = 2, c = 1
19. a = 1, b = 2, c = 3
20. a = 3, b = 2, c = 1

How did you do?

Less than 20: Do the quiz again – you're missing something!

20-30: Call the spiritual ambulance; special care is needed here. You either need a top-up course, you're having a 'bad faith day', or you are exceptionally humble and trying not to show everyone else up! Remedy? Live in church for a while, read lots of Bible, get a prayer therapist.

30-40: OK, you have your spiritual aches and pains, and a bit of forgetfulness, but basically you're in good shape. Keep up with the exercises and try again in a few months' time. Remedy? More of the same. Make sure your spiritual diet is well balanced. Maybe fewer novels and more spiritual books?

40-50: You're the picture of rosy spiritual good health, skipping along saying your prayers, singing hymns and reciting the creed. Be careful, other people might start avoiding you if you come across too holy. Remedy? Stay real, and watch out for the sin of pride. Just when you know you're in the top few per cent spiritually, pride can totally undermine your score and lower your ranking!

50-60: Hey, you with the halo! You're ridiculously spiritually super-charged. Anyone touching you may get a static shock. You won't be invited to any parties in case you start preaching. You are in danger of getting a complex and thinking you are someone you're not. And, sorry to say this, but you actually rank below the 20-30 score group (Matthew 20:16). Commiserations!

All in fun, of course!

Music for meditation

The following are suggested as suitable for quiet reflection, together or alone:

Spiegel im Spiegel – *Arvo Pärt*

Officium (album) – *Jan Garbarek & The Hilliard Ensemble*

Fantasia on a theme of Thomas Tallis – *Vaughan Williams*

The Lark Ascending – *Vaughan Williams*

Due Tramonti – *Einaudi*

Nefeli – *Einaudi*

Concerto for Flute & Harp in C major – *Mozart*

Prelude No. 15 in D flat 'Raindrop' – *Chopin*

Cello Suites, inspired by Bach – *Yo-Yo Ma*

Andante Cantabile (String Quartet no. 1) – *Vytautas Sondeckis/Lithuanian Chamber Orchestra*

Symphony No. 3 – *Górecki*
Pavane Pour Une Infante Défunte – *Fauré*
Symphony No. 8 in D minor 'Unfinished' – *Schubert*